Sim

Flames Across The Tawe

Flames Across The Tawe

The Illustrated History of Swansea City Fire Brigade

by Keith Mills

breedon **books**
PUBLISHING

First published in Great Britain in 2001 by
The Breedon Books Publishing Company Limited
Breedon House, 3 The Parker Centre, Derby, DE21 4SZ.

ISBN 1 85983 202 4

Printed and bound by Butler & Tanner, Frome, Somerset, England.

Jacket printing by GreenShires, Leicester, England.

Contents

Foreword

When the author told me of his intention to research the history of the Swansea Fire Brigade, having scratched the surface many years ago, I knew the time and effort that would be required to gather the information from such a wide range of sources.

The Fire Brigade is a service which has a duty to protect the population, industry and commerce within its area from the effects of fire. In many ways it reflects the development of that area and mirrors the changes and patterns which took place as the town grew from its early days to develop as a city.

Swansea Fire Brigade has faced tremendous challenges during its long history – the Blitz, the famous tanker fires of the 1950s, and then the transition to a complete Emergency and Rescue Service. It has been my privilege to be closely involved in all these aspects during my 40 years of service. This book is a fitting tribute to all who have served in the brigade.

It is fortunate that a history of the brigade has been compiled before some of the elements have been lost or, with the passage of time, become no longer available. I congratulate the author for his time-consuming and painstaking research and the careful selection of material to present this historical record of a fine tradition of service to the City of Swansea.

Leonard Clarke OBE, FIFireE
Chief Fire Officer, Swansea Fire Brigade 1962–1968
Her Majesty's Inspector of Fire Services (Wales and Central England) 1968–1977

Foreword

Having been invited to write a foreword to this publication, it affords me the opportunity to pay tribute to the author, who has spent countless hours in research so necessary to produce such detail.

It is obvious from the reports and photographs that Swansea was well served by its fire service, which is due to the dedicated men and women who served in the brigade.

April 1974 saw the end of the Swansea Fire Brigade, when it was absorbed into the newly-formed West Glamorgan Fire Service, which has since been amalgamated to form the Mid and West Wales Fire Service.

Former members of the old Swansea Fire Brigade continue to serve in the new fire service, and in the true tradition of firefighters, will continue to provide the excellent service which has been their hallmark.

W.F. Dancey OBE, QFSM
Chief Fire Officer Swansea Fire Brigade 1968–1974

Acknowledgements

In researching this book I have received an unbelievable amount of assistance from numerous sources and I record here my sincere gratitude to everyone who not only shared information and loaned photographs – without which the writing of this book would not have been possible – but who also showed interest and enthusiasm for the project throughout the past few years.

I would also like to place on record my sincere thanks to Anton Rippon of Breedon Books for the faith he placed in me, for without that belief the project I undertook would never have come to fruition.

Those who have assisted me include: BBC Broadcasting House in Cardiff; Mrs Marilyn Jones of the Swansea Reference Library's Cambrian Index; Chief Fire Officer Mr G. Edwards and L/Ff. Mark Blatchford, Cornwall Fire Brigade; Cardiff City Central Reference Library; Dowlais Central Library; Dennis Fire Appliances; Driver and Vehicle Licensing Agency; Fire Service Preservation Group; Fire Brigade Society; Mr Alan Gower; Glamorgan Archives, Cardiff; HTV Wales; Mrs Enid John; Mrs Maud Jones; *London Gazette*; Mid and West Wales Fire Service; Mid and West Wales Fire Service Restoration Society, Monuments Room; Surrey Records Office, Guildford; Surrey Records Office, Woking; Mr Spring, Norwich Union Insurance Company; Mrs Sheree Leeds, Public Record Office, Kew, London; Reference Library of the Commonwealth War Graves; South Wales Police Museum; Mr Jeremy Glenn, Curator, Swansea City Reference Library; Swansea City Archives; Dr John Alban; John Maudsley; Gwyn Davies; National Association of Retired Firefighters, West Glamorgan Branch; *South Wales Evening Post*; Swansea Maritime Museum; Gerald Gabb; Mr Anthony Rae; Spink & Son, Medalists, King Street, London; Welsh Area Fire Engine Restoration Society; West Glamorgan Archives; Mr Austin, ex AFS/NFS; Mr Mike Andrews; Mrs Wendy Cope; Mumbles & Oystermouth Historical Society; Mr John Carey, (deceased), ex-SFB; Mr L.O. Clarke, former Chief Fire Officer, SFB; Mr Bill Dancey, former Chief Fire Officer, SFB; Mr A. Davies, ex-SFB; Mr Harry Davies, L/Fm. (deceased), ex-SFB; Mr Gregory Davies; Mr Dennis (Dapper) Davies (deceased), ex-SFB; Mr Arthur Edwards, ex-SFB; Mr Alan Fox, ex-SFB; Mr Jack Fox, (deceased), former Deputy Chief Fire Officer, SFB; Mr Mike George, ex-Mid & West Wales Fire Service; Mr Paul Hopwood, Dennis Fire Appliances; Mr Reg Haley; Mr Pressdee; Mrs Perman; Mr Andrew Quinn, Deputy Chief Fire Officer, Cork Fire Brigade; Mr David Roberts; Mr Derrick Scott; Mr Fred Tingle; Mr Brian Veroid, ex-Norwich Fire Brigade; Mr Fred Waters, (deceased), ex police-fireman; Mr Gary Williams; Mr David Williams.

Finally, I would sincerely like to thank my wife, Pam, for the endless hours she had to spend without my company, and my family and friends for their frequent enquiries into the progress of the book, and for their encouragement throughout the years, especially at times when my enthusiasm looked like waning.

Introduction

Following my retirement from the fire service in 1992, I decided to research the history of the Swansea Fire Brigade, which I had joined in 1964. With precious little literature relating to the subject, it was a daunting task. However, thanks to the assistance of numerous individuals I was able to uncover an unbelievable amount of information and many photographs, all of which spurred me on.

In the 1800s, Swansea was a thriving seaport and industrial town and, because of this, it was to encounter several large outbreaks of fire, from factory blazes to ship fires in the docks. In those early years, fires would have been fought with manual fire-engines, which sometimes required as many as 20 men to operate them. They would have been mostly local townspeople, who would be paid with tokens. From the manual fire-engines of the 1800s, Swansea in the 1900s was to see steam and eventually its first motorised fire-engine in 1915.

In its early years, Swansea was covered by police-firemen, who from 1938, following the Fire Services Act, were ably assisted by auxiliary firemen until August 1941, when the National Fire Service was formed. April 1948 saw the formation of the County Borough of Swansea Fire Brigade, which was to run for 26 years until local government re-organisation in 1974 saw it amalgamated into the newly-formed West Glamorgan Fire Service.

I hope that this book will give an insight into the dedication, courage – and on occasions the sheer heroism – of Swansea's firefighters down the years.

Keith Mills
Swansea, 2001

Chapter One

Limited Resources

Following the Great Fire of London, which began on Sunday 2 September 1666, insurance companies began to form their own fire brigades. As more companies came into business, the insurance brigades multiplied. The companies spread throughout the country and the Norwich Union Insurance, although not formed until 1797, set up fire brigades in several towns and cities, erecting its own purpose-built fire stations. Its firemen were dressed in resplendent uniforms, quite impractical for the hazardous job of fighting fire, and a strict disciplinary code relating to the firemen's conduct was introduced. The Norwich Union provided Swansea with fire engines and other equipment to fight local blazes on several occasions. No record exists, however, that they ever established a fire brigade in the town.

The first mention of a fire engine in Swansea came in the local *Cambrian* newspaper on 31 March 1809. The report relates to a fire that had occurred in Castle Lane, at the shop of a Mr Harwood, a grocer and candle maker. Tallow and other materials had ignited and the report comments 'we trust that the inhabitants will no longer suffer the town's engines to remain in their present state.'

Thus we can assume that Swansea was in possession of more than one fire engine, and with no disciplined body responsible for their general maintenance, they would probably not have been examined until required in the event of a fire. With the Swansea Borough Police Force not being established until April 1836, this, and other fires in the borough, would probably have been extinguished by the local townsfolk acting as volunteers, and possibly the military who were garrisoned in nearby Swansea Castle.

Although there is no record of the make of the fire engines kept in Swansea at that time, we can be sure that they were of the manual type. Under normal circumstances it could take up to 22 men to operate the pumping handles, and with the main body of the engine needing to be constantly topped up with water to maintain a jet at the nozzle, many more pairs of hands were required to supply a bucket chain for that purpose.

Following mention of the Castle Lane fire in 1809, there seems to be no reference to fire-engines until a letter to the *Cambrian* in November 1816:

> When we are made aware of the serious state of the town's engines, and that perhaps the inhabitants of Swansea pay a rate of a penny per month for their maintenance, that certain persons appointed to attend them in case of necessity, and take them out at least once a month for the exercise and public inspection, those men, say three to an engine, to have a yearly allowance, which with the expense of keeping the engine in good repair.

There is little information relating to fires within Swansea until a report in the *Cambrian* newspaper on 22 May 1819: 'A powerful Fire Engine of the second size, manufactured by Messrs Hopwood and Tilley of London, has been sent to Swansea by the Norwich Union Insurance Company for the use of the town.' However, the Board Minute Book of the Norwich Union Insurance Company states: '18th March 1822. Ordered: that the engine, buckets and other effects in the undermentioned district belonging to the Old Society, be purchased for this society. Swansea Engine, Buckets, Hose, &c £71 13s 6d.'

The 'Old Society' simply means the Norwich Union Insurance Company, prior to its re-organisation in 1821. With regard to this statement from the Norwich Union archives, it is possible that the Company may have purchased two manual fire-engines for Swansea. Although the Norwich Union was established in 1797, there are no records prior to 1821. In March 1822, incidentally, the Shand Mason catalogue stated that a horse-drawn curricle engine for 22 men cost £78.

In January 1836, at a meeting of Swansea's inhabitants presided over by Revd Dr Hewson, there was once again general concern about the state of the town's fire engines, and the opinion was voiced that the Norwich Union engine was insufficient. Three years earlier, the sum of £10 had been received from the Norwich Union for repairs to the body of its engine. Now it was felt that there was need for an extra, or at least larger, engine for Swansea. This had come about after two serious fires, one at the premises of Mr Francis, coach manufacturer, and the other on board the brig *Martha* in the dock. The outcome of the meeting was that the Vestry Clerk was directed to apply to different insurance companies to contribute towards the cost of a new fire engine. Consequently, the Royal Exchange Insurance Company wrote to the Town Council, offering the sum of 20 guineas (£21) towards that cost.

However, concerns over Swansea's ability to fight fire were to continue and the editor of the *Cambrian* received several letters from the general public offering their recommendations for personnel to act as firemen. There were suggestions that firemen should be dressed in appropriate uniforms, and one writer said that in the event of a fire, the said personnel should be summoned by the tolling of a bell, which would be situated on a building converted to act as a 'fire station', suitably marked with a name plate over its main door. An engineer should also act as a keyholder and reside on the premises.

Other ideas included a 'fire-float' which would involve a force pump being attached to the deck of a steam tug for use in the docks and river, in effect a 'floating fire engine', to be used in the event of a fire on board a vessel, or in one of the dockside warehouses. Many writers stressed that under no circumstances should the police be expected to act as firemen, as they would be busy enough attempting to keep the peace, thus enabling the 'specialist' firemen to go about the job of extinguishing the blaze.

These concerns, however, went unheeded. Although the Borough Police Force had only been established in April 1836 – and at that time had only one inspector and six constables – the Town Council was still against forming a fire brigade, and as a result the responsibility remained with the police.

However, public concern about a properly-established fire brigade was never far away, and in November 1837, at a meeting of the Town Council, the provision of a building for the storing of Swansea's fire engines was discussed. It was decided that the ground floor of the Town Hall (situated at that time on ground adjacent to the castle) should be converted for that purpose. The building was also to be used as a police station, and the plans were thought to be an ideal arrangement.

In 1838, Swansea was to see the establishment of 'fire plugs', a means of drawing water from the town's mains and the forerunner of today's fire hydrants. This was to prove a great asset to the firemen, although obtaining water from the mains was no mean feat, as a wooden plug had to be withdrawn from the main and a standpipe inserted to produce the supply for the engine. This, however, had to be achieved while the main was charged and under pressure. The process required two firemen, one to remove the wooden plug from the mains (this was achieved with the use of a large spiked lever), the other to insert the standpipe. As one can imagine, the operation always ended with the two firemen concerned being soaked through even before they attempted to extinguish the fire.

Despite the lack of records to suggest that the Norwich Union Insurance Company established a fire brigade in Swansea, a report from an agent of the Norwich Union stated in the *Cambrian* in 1838:

> The agent takes this opportunity of stating that the Office having sent him down a first-class fire engine, it is his intention to appoint a Fire Brigade, consisting of 21 men, which he will take upon his command in person, in order that they may be as effective a Corps as that of the London. The men will be known by some distinguishing badge or mark, each man will be required to place over his door the word 'FIREMAN'. A list of their names will be left at the Police Station where the engine is kept, the keys of which will be left with some respectable inhabitants residing near the Station House.
>
> Under these circumstances, the Agent begs respectfully to solicit an increased support from the enlightened and liberal inhabitants of this town and neighbourhood.
>
> Geo. T. Stroud
> (Agent) Norwich Union & Life Office
> Mount Street
> Swansea
> September 1st 1838

Extensive research into archives both at Swansea and the Norwich Union has uncovered nothing of the above-mentioned George T. Stroud's aspiration to establish a fire brigade in Swansea. In November 1842, however, a house fire at the Union Buildings, Swansea, was attended by Constable Robert Williams, whose prompt action and efficient assistance averted a serious fire. The same constable, along with PC Webb, one of Swansea's first police officers in 1836, attended a fire at Danygraig House. On their arrival, however, they found that the fire, which had started in the laundry, was nearly subdued.

In May 1843, Swansea was thrown into turmoil when a serious fire occurred in the Strand, near Green Dragon Lane. The fire was discovered at 1am by a passing constable who ran to the Station House to raise the alarm. The turncock, a Mr Marshall, was alerted and soon the powerful first-class engine of the Norwich Union was at the scene at Messrs Couch's warehouse, along with a detachment of the 73rd Regiment, under the command of Captain Widderington, and a Mr Lyons, together with 'an efficient body of police and other able-bodied men'. The report goes on to say that by this time the fire, which was now burning quite fiercely, had spread to the adjoining building of Mr Beynon, whose premises were filled with combustible materials such as canvas, rope, oakum – and even a quantity of gunpowder. By 2am, although the Norwich engine was pouring a continual supply of water into the buildings, all hope of saving them was gone.

The panic of those living nearby can only be imagined and a large number began to remove furniture and belongings from their houses for fear of the fire spreading, especially when word got round that gunpowder was stored in Beynon's warehouse. Not surprisingly, this news also deterred several people from taking an active part in attempting to extinguish the flames. Their anxieties were hardly relieved when there were two or three explosions and part of the roof collapsed.

Norwich Union fireman of the 19th century, posing in his resplendent, but impractical, uniform. (Norwich Union Archives)

With the Norwich engine still pouring large quantities of water on to the blazing buildings (remember, it required 22 men to operate the pumping handles), the Hafod engine arrived and joined the struggle. By this time the flames were so great that they lit up the Swansea skyline and could be seen from a great distance. Embers fell on house roofs in the Wind Street, Fisher Street and Frog Street districts, and soon the whole of the Couch and Beynon warehouses had been consumed.

In the aftermath of the fire, the *Cambrian* published two letters, one each from Messrs Couch and Beynon, the owners of the buildings destroyed, expressing their sincere thanks to all concerned for their assistance. The Town Council resolved that a dinner be given to honour the 73rd Regiment for their work, and also that £20 be distributed among all those who took an active part during the outbreak. The payment was divided thus: 10s (50p) to each man who had been on the roofs of the buildings, 5s (25p) to all those who had worked the engine, and 2s 6d (12½p) to those who had 'made themselves useful'.

At a later police meeting the mayor informed those present that the Vivians at Singleton Abbey had offered the use of their engine, should it ever be required.

Even at this time the Swansea engine was, in turn, helping neighbouring local authorities. In the small hours of a June day in 1843, for instance, it turned out to a large, destructive fire which had gripped the Vale of Neath Brewery. Although the Neath and Neath Abbey engines were already in attendance, valuable time had been lost in getting water on to the flames because the hose on the Neath engine was not in good working order. The building was a vast pyramid of flames, and although special praise was given to those attempting to subdue the blaze, the fire still burned practically unchecked. Just after 4am, a messenger was despatched to ask for help from Swansea. After a delay of almost an hour while they obtained horses, the Swansea engine got to the fire in 45 minutes, only to find that their assistance was no longer required as the blaze had been extinguished.

The year 1843 was a busy time for the fire brigade in Swansea, and because of serious public and Council concern about providing sufficient fire brigade personnel, as well as the efficiency of the engines, a Mr Smith was sent to London to visit several fire engine manufacturers. Patterns of the largest-sized engines were exhibited to the Council, who were told that these large engines would each require 40 men to work them at a cost of £190. It seems a coincidence, but at a Police Committee meeting in August of that year, a sub-committee was appointed to select 40 townspeople to act as a fire brigade. Although the resolution to establish a fire brigade had been passed, there were no actual reports of one being formed, and in a Town Council meeting in January 1846 mention was once again made of the condition of the town's fire engine and equipment. The Council minutes tell us that a Mr John Morgan of Park Street, Swansea, had been required to inform the Police Committee of the reason for the town's engine and hose being in a poor condition. The report stated that the equipment had been '... allowed to get into so mouldy, rusty and deteriorated a condition, that had fire occurred in the town, their services would have been almost unavailing.' The Committee went on to chastise Mr Morgan for his failure to oil the hose, (at this time, the hose was made of leather and required constant oiling to prevent it cracking and keep it supple) and for neglecting to taken out the engine for inspection and operation.

Blame was also attributed to Inspector Rees for his use of a small pipe (nozzle) when 16 men had been employed in pumping the engine. Undue pressure had been exerted on the poorly maintained hose, thus encouraging the hose to burst. The Council meeting was protracted, with accusations passing back and forth of incidents relating to defective hoses at other outbreaks. The eventual recommendation of the Council was to dismiss Mr Morgan, and pass responsibility for all future maintenance of the engine, hose and equipment to Inspector Rees.

Three years later, on 18 September 1846, Inspector William Rees and his men were called to a rick fire in Heathfield Terrace, Swansea. When they arrived with the engine they were ably assisted by local inhabitants, military personnel and Water Works employees who were watering the streets nearby. Considering that when the borough police force was established ten years earlier it consisted of only seven personnel, and that since then there had been no substantial increase in manpower, it is hardly surprising that the police sometimes had to rely on the assistance of the townsfolk and others when attending fires.

Some two months later, on 13 November 1846, when a fire broke out in Wind Street, 'not withstanding every exertions, it was found impossible to work two engines owing to the shortness of the hose'. After the incident, Mr O.G. Williams told the Town Council that not only was the hose deficient, but the small engine was in need of repair. Once again a debt of gratitude was owed to civilians and the 53rd Regiment for helping with the firefighting.

With the borough police force still relatively small in numbers, it was inevitable that during an outbreak of fire they would encounter difficulties. Although this was recognised by some councillors and townsfolk, very little practically was done. The ongoing debate, which followed most fires, continued.

Then on Sunday 2 September 1848, a serious fire occurred at the hairdressers shop of Mr Richards, in the vicinity of High Street, Castle Street and Gower Street. The shop was soon engulfed in flames, and the occupants, Mr Richards and his family, had to flee the building and take refuge in the nearby Cameron Arms. The alarm was raised, and PC Noah Owen was first on the scene, closely followed by Messrs Glover, Rogers and Inspector Rees, as well as Mr W.H. Smith of the Water Works Company and several others. As there were only two policemen at the scene, it seems likely that the engines, which arrived later, were brought up by other members of the force. The report of the fire states that after the arrival of the engines, it proved very difficult to obtain a good supply of water from the mains. For a considerable period of time the effort to extinguish the fire consisted of bucket chains from neighbouring houses. With a Water Works official already in attendance, the necessary valves for diverting the towns mains to the vicinity of the fire had been operated, but despite these efforts there was still a lack of supply. Eventually it became clear that the standpipe that was fixed into the main to feed the engine was only partially open. According to an eyewitness, this led to a delay of an hour or more, which probably contributed to the total destruction of Mr Richards' premises and considerable damage to the adjoining building, belonging to Mr West the tailor.

At a meeting of the town's inhabitants, it was decided to form a committee to confer with the Town Council to discuss again the possibility of establishing a fire brigade. The members elected to serve on the committee were: P. and L. Grenfell, J.G. Jefferies, David Francis, William Clarke, David Walters, J. Hoare, William Stroud and Revd C.R. Jones. When the committee met with the Town Council a week later, the mayor, who opened the meeting with his own views on the establishment of a town fire brigade, said: 'That he did not believe that the town would benefit from the establishment of a fire brigade, for this reason, that in a few years it would become a dead letter, perhaps, for four or five years it would go on pretty well, but they would find after the brigade was formed, some would die, whilst others would leave the town, and thus it would soon become "none est investus".'

If a brigade were to be appointed, he thought that they ought not to be a body of men kept in constant training. He considered that a settled body like the police force, who were always ready and under command on the spot, could do the job more effectively than a fire brigade like the one sought by the deputation.

Although the deputation had attended the meeting well prepared, even to the extent of outlining what format the brigade should take, including its pay and rank structure, the Council remained unmoved. During the past ten years, only seven or eight fires had occurred in the borough, and the Council could not expect the inhabitants of Swansea to pay further taxes to fund the provision of a fire brigade. However, they did conclude that they should employ an experienced and competent person to maintain the fire engine and its apparatus at the police station. This, along with the services of the police and the military, who attended most serious fires, meant that Swansea did not need its own fire brigade.

The argument continued, as Mr William Stroud, of the inhabitants committee, pointed out the delay and difficulties that had arisen at the recent High Street and other previous fires. The Council replied that they did not agree that the neglect and ignorance of some people attending the recent fires was sufficient reason to agree to the proposed plan. Mr O.G. Williams of the Council also suggested that although the Norwich Union Insurance Company had kept a fire engine in the town for a number of years, all the other insurance companies which were supported in the town should be contacted, with a view to them forming their own insurance brigade.

Mr William Stroud, although he had been quite meticulous in his plans for the establishment of a fire brigade in Swansea, was ultimately unsuccessful in his attempts, much like his namesake, George T. Stroud, an agent of the Norwich Union, ten years earlier.

During the next few years the Council did introduce measures to prevent fires in the town. The Paving Commission located and identified the fire plugs situated around the town by providing wall plates to mark their whereabouts.

Today these are known as hydrant plates. It was hoped that this would reduce the delay in firemen locating fire plugs in the event of fire.

In December 1853, the Town Council were informed by a Mr George Allen of the Birmingham Fire Office that his company were making a gift of 'that Company's most powerful fire engine.' On 30 March 1854, the Birmingham Fire Office fire engine was tested in various parts of the town. The engine was said to be of the first-class type approved construction, drawn by four horses. The make of the engine is not specified. Those present at the testing were the Swansea Borough Police Force under Superintendent Tate, along with members of the Birmingham Fire Office Fire Brigade under the command of Superintendent Mr Sutton, all of whom were dressed in their resplendent insurance office uniforms.

The issue of establishing a fire brigade in the town was once again brought to the fore in November 1855, when a serious fire occurred on the premises of Messrs Matthews Bros in Castle Square. The fire was first noticed by Mr and Mrs Roe of the Ship public house at about 1.10am, when they observed smoke issuing from the building. On discovering the outbreak they let out cries of 'Fire!' and 'Police!', and this alarm reached the ears of the nearest policeman, Sergeant Noah Owen. On reaching the premises he burst open the door, only to observe that the whole back portion of the premises was engulfed in a mass of flames. He immediately ran to the nearby police station to raise the alarm, leaving Mr Roe in charge of alerting the people inside the building. Fortunately by this time Mr Roe had been joined by Sergeant Lewis, who made several attempts to enter the building, only to be driven back by the intense heat and smoke.

The ominous sound of the town's 'fire bell' rang out, along with shouts of 'Fire!', which echoed through the streets. The rumble of the fire engines and the heavy tread of policemen's boots could be also be heard. The night sky was illuminated by the glare of the fire, and in a short space of time a mass of people had gathered at the scene to watch people escaping from the upper floors of the Matthews' establishment. First was Mr Bliss, the assistant, who was descended from the first-floor window by means of a knotted bed sheet. He was followed by the housekeeper, who was overcome by danger and exhaustion. Mr Matthews had to hold on to her until a Mr Stevens, a plumber, brought a ladder which

enabled them both to descend to the street below. Three other assistants who had been asleep in the attic, finding escape by the staircase impossible, resorted to climbing out through the skylight and over the roof into Mr Richmond's skylight, from which they were able to make good their escape. By this time the whole front of the building was in flames.

The first engine had arrived on the scene approximately 15 minutes after the alarm had been raised, followed five minutes later by the second engine. The fire plugs were removed and the standpipes fixed into the mains, but no water was forthcoming. As the fire burned unchecked, the scene was described as one of awful grandeur. The turncock, a Mr Rees, continued to attempt to draw water from the main, re-directing the flow by operating various street valves, but the flames raged freely for some 40 minutes, and the only means of subduing them was by a bucket chain, using water from public pumps in Goat Street and College Street.

To add to the confusion the gas supply for the street lighting was extinguished, which unfortunately allowed certain individuals to make off with some of the property that had been rescued from the inferno. With the fire spreading to the adjoining properties of Mr Jonathan Owen, the jeweller, and on the lower side, the drapery establishment of Mr Thomas Richmond, the 'Birmingham' engine was taken to the Strand. It was unable to draw water from the Strand mains without diminishing the supply to Castle Square. This was overcome by the formation of a bucket chain to extract a supply from the nearby float (dock).

A further delay was encountered when the fire hose on the Birmingham engine burst. The hose was described as being 'rotten as a pear,' and its loss rendered the engine unworkable. Many working-class men and women joined in to help move water after the engine failed, and they eventually checked the flames on one side of the Matthews premises. By this time all hope of saving the Matthews' property

A curricle street fire escape ladder of the 1800s, a forerunner to the escape ladders carried on fire appliances well into the 1970s. This particular ladder came from the Penrice Estate, Gower, and was donated to the Mid & West Wales Fire Service Preservation Group by Mr Methuen Campbell. (Author's collection)

was given up, and the police directed their exertions to preventing the flames from spreading to the adjoining properties. At one time during the blaze, three men, Mr Jerry Rosser, Mr Radford and one other, came forward to assist. They climbed on to the roof of one of the buildings and succeeded in using a rope to haul aloft a length of hose. Sergeant David Lewis took a stand between the properties. By this time a reasonable supply of water had been obtained, and the fire was prevented from spreading further. Constable Taylor fell off a ladder and injured his leg.

The flames were finally subdued at 6am, although smoke continued to rise from the ruins during Sunday. For safety reasons the walls of the Matthews property were eventually demolished.

After the fire a report concluded that 'The engines on the spot were the Norwich, the Corporation and Birmingham, under the control and general directions of Superintendent Tate, whose services on this occasion, as well as those of the Police Force, have

elicited the praise and approbation of the authorities.' Along with the mention of praise, there was to follow general criticism of those responsible for firefighting, namely the Town Council and the police fire brigade. The report read:

Many of them indeed worked nobly and cheerfully and in many instances, encountered considerable personal danger. But when we say this much, we cannot shut our eyes to the fact that there was throughout great confusion, very little method, and a painful want of organisation on this occasion. This was patent to most present, and a subject for general remark. For this we do not for a moment mean to blame either the Superintendent or his men, for what took place at the time arose entirely from a defective plan of operations, a plan emanating from the collective wisdom of the Swansea Town Council, who seem to imagine that, in cases of fire, Police regulations are unnecessary, by the convertibility of our Police into an improvised Fire Brigade. There never was a greater mistake. There never was a stronger illustration of it than during the fire. We hear of one Policeman on the summit of the buildings plying water when others are looking on, another peddling with the hose of the engine, about which he knows nothing, another pumping here and another there, we are naturally led to ask, in sober earnestness, are these the duties of policemen in a great emergency like this? We say emphatically no, when a fire rages, property is exposed, and hundreds are present, proper police regulations are of the last consequence. The crowd should be kept off, the engines should have room to play, the exposed premises should be watched, and properly protected. Who is to do these things if our Town Council expect the Police only to attend the engines? On Sunday morning, houses were forced open indiscriminately, property was stolen, and furniture and goods hurled into the street as if they were completely valueless. We say it was the obvious duty of the Police to prevent this, and protect property, and leave the engines to be worked by parties who should as usual, be remunerated for their trouble. Had this been done, more good would have been effected, had the crowds been kept back, and a cordon formed in front of the exposed premises, there would have been less confusion, better organisation, more work done, and considerably less destruction.

Following this report into the fire at Castle Square, the Town Council received a barrage of letters of complaint from the general public by way of the local press, so much so that a committee was formed by the Council to listen to the complaints of the townspeople at a meeting. The complaints raised at the meeting echoed those included in the report. The townspeople called on the Council to establish a fire brigade for the town, and even submitted a document suggesting what format it should take. The Town Council's reply was of no real value, as they stressed once again that the police would take the responsibility of acting as the fire brigade.

Twelve months later, on 10 October 1856, another serious fire occurred at a furniture warehouse belonging to a Mr Fuller, of 231 High Street. Once again the police encountered difficulty in securing a good supply of water. Once a good supply was eventually forthcoming, the police were left with the task of saving the adjoining buildings, the Bush Hotel and the premises of Mr W.H. Michael, as the warehouse belonging to Mr Fuller had been totally consumed. Present at the fire, along with Superintendent Tate of the police, were the mayor and Mr George Turton Stroud, agent for the Norwich Union Insurance Company, who had already attempted to establish a fire brigade in Swansea in September 1838. On several occasions insurance company agents attended fires, and some were even involved in directing operations along with the town councillors, possibly looking after their company's interests. Some of these agents were Mr M.J. Michael of the Alliance, Mr Oakshot of London Assurance, Mr Martin of Royal Exchange, Mr Arnold of the Birmingham and Mr G.T. Stroud of the Norwich Union. The Birmingham and the Norwich Union supplied two of the town's fire engines.

When he gave the police report on the fire, Superintendent Tate informed the meeting that during the fire there had been interference by some persons present, who gave their own orders and obstructed the police in their duties. He believed that these people were acting on orders from their superiors. It is unclear who Superintendent Tate was referring to in his statement – it could have been the town councillors, or the insurance agents themselves. The superintendent's report went on to say that he had directed all constables to take no orders except those from the official authorities. The council were further informed that he had encountered some resistance from the working classes, when they were requested to operate the pumps. 'Who is to pay us', they shouted, and 'We are willing to work if we get paid.' The superintendent had taken upon himself the responsibility of reassuring them, by replying 'Work away and I will see you get paid', which had procured ample assistance. Superintendent Tate stated that it was important that assistance given at fires should be promptly rewarded.

He concluded his report by informing the meeting that he had recently brought out the engines and exercised and instructed the whole force, especially those who had recently joined, in the working of the engines, hose and ladders. He had also ensured 'that they were in good working order and state of repair.'

In the ensuing discussion the mayor informed the meeting that Mr G.T. Stroud of the Norwich Union Insurance Company reported that his company would be giving the sum of £20 to distribute among those that had assisted at the fire.

At a Town Council meeting in February 1858, Mr Stroud addressed the Council and enquired into the condition of the town's fire engines. Superintendent Dunn (who had just been appointed following the retirement of Superintendent Henry Tate), replied that he had not been aware that he was to be superintendent of the fire brigade before taking up his post of superintendent of police in Swansea, and that it was not a duty he was familiar with. The mayor then informed Mr Stroud that Inspector Bennett, who had been attending to the fire engines, would continue to give them his attention with the aid of the superintendent, who would also take charge of organising an effective fire brigade without additional expense to the borough.

In the early hours of Saturday 3 April 1858 a serious fire broke out at the premises of a Mr Arkell at 60 Wind Street. Another delay in drawing water from the mains forced police and townspeople to stand and watch as the fire consumed the property of Mr Arkell, a boot maker, and Mr W.H. Spring, his neighbour. When the engine arrived and the standpipe was fixed, the water supply was exhausted after 10 or 12 strokes of the pumping handles. It was another 45 minutes before an adequate supply was available, and by this time both properties had been gutted. The mayor, Mr G.T. Stroud and other officials were in attendance, and witnessed first hand the problems encountered by the police in extinguishing the flames, including the refusal of some able-bodied labourers to assist.

At the fortnightly Council meeting on 16 April 1858 the mayor, Mr W.H. Michael, informed those present of the difficulties that had arisen at the recent fire in Wind Street, and said that the Council could no longer refrain from equipping the town with the means of defending itself against fire. He recommended that serious thought be given to purchasing a wheeled escape ladder, and that an approach should be made to the various insurance companies, to encourage them to contribute to the cost of establishing a fire brigade for the town. He was further concerned about the crime that accompanied a fire. The mayor also reported that after the fire several tradesmen had expressed their willingness to organise a fire brigade, all of whom resided close to the police station. As far as the water supply was concerned, he had been informed that following repairs to the Uplands reservoir, the High Street main would always be kept charged, and could, even without the assistance of the engine, throw a jet of water over nearly every house in the town. Councillor E.M. Richards remarked that the improvements put forward by the mayor had been brought before the Council on previous occasions, but had been allowed to drop because of a lack of funds to carry them further. The seriousness of the situation meant that the time had come to address the matter.

After a lengthy discussion, Mr Richards resolved that a recommendation be put to the Local Board of Health to procure an escape ladder, and that a committee consisting of the mayor and Messrs Jenkin, Oakshot, Stroud and Hoare be formed to report on what arrangements could be made to organise a fire brigade for the borough.

Attending a meeting at the end of April, the mayor informed the Local Board of Health that he intended to call a special meeting of the committee, and confer with the agents of the various insurance companies, with the view to advancing the fire brigade project. Even the Government Inspector of Police, Captain Willis, added his voice to those who were concerned about the police being employed as a fire brigade.

The debate about whether Swansea was to have an established fire brigade continued, and meanwhile fires continued to break out. On 3 July 1858 another serious fire occurred, this time at 1 Wind Street, in the opticians shop of Mr Bryant Biggs. The Norwich engine was already attending another fire in Wassail Square when the tolling of the newly erected fire bell on the police station was sounded. The Birmingham engine responded, and was joined soon afterwards by the Norwich, which had quickly extinguished the small fire in Wassail Square. The Wind Street fire had by this time had taken a good hold of the premises. A lack of water for the fire crews meant that police and civilians could only stand by powerless as the valuable property was sacrificed to the fire. The fire reached the first and second storeys, and by the time a plentiful supply of water became available all hopes of saving Mr Biggs's house had faded. All that could be done was to confine the flames and save the adjoining properties.

By now it had become customary to conduct a post-mortem in the local press on the fires that had occurred in the town, with letters to the editor being quite common. One such letter read:

> We very much regret to say, that some of the light fingered gentry were very busily engaged in plying their 'profession' during the fire, and the number of robberies of watches, purses etc. committed are almost incredible. By reference to our Police report it will be seen that some eight or nine suspicious characters have been locked up, charged with being concerned in those robberies, and although the Superintendent was unable to bring together sufficient legal evidence to convict them upon, still their 'sport' was spoiled for the regatta, as they were kept in custody over these days.

Statements like this added fuel to the arguments about the role of the police at fires. Inspector Brooks, in his report into the fire at Mr Biggs's opticians shop in Wind Street, said that the 'whole Police Force of the Borough' was in attendance and fighting the fire, a fact which only served to fuel concern about the capacity of the police to act as firemen.

The letters in the local press continued, and some townsfolk volunteered to act as firemen. The Town Council purchased a 60ft wheeled escape ladder from the Royal Society for the Preservation of Life, at a cost of £60 including transport. This, the Council concluded, would be kept alongside Temple Street Police Station for use in the event of fire. At a further Council meeting they issued a set of rules and guidelines for use by a fire brigade. The mayor, Mr W.H. Michael, informed the Committee that the insurance companies in the town were generally unwilling to contribute annually to funding or maintaining a fire brigade in Swansea. The mayor went on to state that although the Council had received this refusal, he felt that provision should nevertheless be made for establishing a fire brigade.

Some of the councillors present, who were also businessmen in the town, were so incensed by the insurance companies refusal to contribute that they were prepared to boycott those companies and transfer their policies to those that would contribute to the running of a fire brigade.

The Committee drew up a set of guidelines for the establishment of a fire brigade. These were:

1. To keep the engines, hose etc. in proper repair.
2. To have some responsible person appointed to direct all operations for extinguishing fires and using the engines.
3. To have a body of men trained to such use, who should act under the direction of the Superintendent, associated with the Surveyor of the Local Board of Health.
4. To enable the Police Force to be kept to its own special duties, namely, to secure order, to keep off undue pressure by the crowd, to enable the engines to be properly worked and to protect property.

On 23 July 1858, a serious fire occurred at Neath, at the premises of a Mr William Williams, an ironmonger in Green Street. The Neath, Neath Abbey and the Vale of Neath Brewery fire engines attended, but even with an ample supply of water, the engines were too small to cope. Within a short time the fire had spread to the adjoining grocers and drapers shops. Superintendent Parsons of the Neath Police immediately sent a telegraphic message to Superintendent Dunn of the Swansea Force, requesting the assistance of the Swansea Fire Brigade. Horses were requisitioned from Mr Williams's livery stables in Fisher Street and the Birmingham engine was dispatched from Swansea, crewed by Superintendent Dunn, Inspector Brooks, Sergeant Crockford, Constable George Williams, a Mr Woolacott and Mr Stevens, a plumber from Wind Street.

The journey from Swansea to Neath took an incredible 50 minutes, and on arrival the engine and crew were met with cheering, clapping and even had the odd bucket of water thrown over them. Although by this time the fire was somewhat subdued, it was far from extinguished, and the effect of the Swansea engine, once it had obtained a good supply of water, was considerable. It played jets through the second-storey windows, right into the heart of the flames, preventing the fire from spreading further into the adjoining premises. All that remained of Mr Williams's ironmongers were bare walls. The building was totally destroyed.

Superintendent Lynn, in his report to Neath Council, stated that as far back as May he had informed the Council of the state of the Neath engine. The 'buckets were out of repair, the hose dirty and impliable and the engine was used as a hen roost.' Swansea was not alone in struggling with dilapidated and ill-maintained equipment.

The crew that attended the Neath fire was augmented by two civilians, Mr Woolacott and Mr Stevens the plumber. Mr Stevens had previously provided a ladder and assisted in the rescue of Mr Matthews and his housekeeper from the fire in Castle Square in November 1855.

Superintendent Dunn voiced his concern about police involvement in fighting fires to the Committee at the monthly council meeting. He was of the opinion that the Council should proceed with the appointment of a superintendent and a body of four or five men to man the engines and take over the responsibilities of a fire brigade.

The concerns of the superintendent and some councillors were heeded, and in October 1858 at a Fire Brigade Committee meeting, Superintendent Dunn handed the Council a list of nine men that he believed should form the fire brigade. The matter was referred to the mayor, to appoint the men and take the necessary steps to establish a fully-functioning fire brigade. This, it is believed, is the first record of the formation of a fire brigade. The mayor's retirement speech, on 12 December 1858, made reference to this achievement.

With regard to the past year, although he had not been able to witness those improvements in the town which he had hoped to see, yet he was happy to think that, before retiring from office, he had been the means of establishing some arrangement for checking the ravages of fire, in the purchase of a fire escape and the formation of a fire brigade, and it was not the least strange coincidence that the escape and the fire brigade should have been brought into requisition for the first time, and should have been the means of saving papers and property to the value of thousands of pounds belonging to the gentleman who had that day been elected mayor.

At the inaugural meeting of the new Fire Brigade Committee on 3 December 1858, the retiring mayor, Mr W.H. Michael, was elected Chairman. The meeting went on to resolve that each fireman should be supplied with a helmet, boots, a coat, a lamp, a belt and an axe, and that an order should be sent to Messrs Pearce & Co. of Hart Street, London, for the requisite articles. The superintendent of the fire brigade, Mr John Morgan of Waterloo Street, submitted an order for equipment and fittings for the ladders and engines. An estimate of £9 13s 6d was provided from a J. Holloway for painting and cleaning. The words 'Norwich Union' would be painted on that engine, and dies would be obtained for stamping the buckets and other property 'SFB'. It was also resolved that the Town Surveyor should report on the cost of erecting a shed for the housing of the engines in the old barrack yard (within the confines of the castle).

The costs incurred by the fire brigade at the recent fire at Mr J.T. Jenkin's property in the High Street were also discussed. The total was £12 10s 6d, two-thirds of which (£8 8s 0d) would be applied for to the West of England Insurance Office, while the remainder, £2 2s 0d, would be applied for from the other insurance companies: the Royal Exchange, the Star Life and the Guardian Fire & Life Office. Even though the insurance companies had refused the

Council's request to pay for the maintenance and running of a fire brigade, they were still expected to pay toward the fire brigade when attending fires at properties insured by them.

Some councillors remained sceptical that the fire brigade could operate separately from the police, and feared that the brigade would be a drain on the town's rates. This view was reinforced when the Fire Brigade Committee requested £150 for the purchase of kit and equipment needed to establish the fire brigade. The Chairman, Mr Michael, stressed that the amount was a one-off expense, required for fire-fighting equipment to launch the new service.

On 29 July 1859, a letter from a Mr Sydney Hall appeared in the *Cambrian* newspaper, expressing his appreciation to Superintendent Dunn of the police; Mr Morgan and his men, the fire brigade; and a Captain Herbert and his men who had helped operate the floating fire engine. All those mentioned had attended a fire in the Patent Fuel Works, on the Strand.

The *Cambrian* newspaper reported on 29 October 1859 that the Swansea Fire Brigade had celebrated its first anniversary on 8 October 1858. The celebration took place at the Compass Inn in Goat Street, and the superintendent of the fire brigade, Mr John Morgan, was in the chair. An annual report of the fire brigade was read, in which it was stated that there had been 16 fires since the formation of the brigade on 8 October 1858. The first fire attended was on 12 October in the Harbour Offices. Mr Morgan and his men had attended, but they were not fully familiar with the engine and equipment. They did, however, render valuable assistance, proving their worth by preventing the flames from spreading and saving valuable documents. The report outlined the costs incurred at the fires attended by the brigade. Property destroyed and damage done during seven of the fires amounted to £1,720, but it was impossible to assess the amount of damage done at the remaining nine blazes, including the Harbour Offices, Goat Street School, Wimbush, Grocer, Railway Sheds, Mr

Meager's dock, and the Patent Fuel Works, (not insured). The estimated damage was £2,000. The most recent fire in the town was at Fisher's & Crabb's, High Street. Property insured in the various offices for nine of the fires amounted to £4,950, while the remaining seven were uninsured.

On 30 March 1860 the brigade, now in its second year, was summoned to a serious fire at Mr Burleigh's leather factors in Calvert Street. The report stated that the fire brigade were on the spot in an incredibly short space of time, along with Superintendent Dunn and members of the police. The fire brigade secured a good and plentiful supply of water, and the engine, which was in capital working order, was manfully and energetically worked. The fire was confined to the house of origin.

The debate about Swansea's water supply was to continue, as Mr Burke, chairman of the Sanitary Committee, and Mr Michael, of the Fire Brigades Committee, both complained about the lack of water for their respective needs. Swansea's population at this time was estimated at 50,000, and there was a growing need for additional, larger reservoirs, and renewal of town mains. In certain parts of the town, especially in the higher regions, the people were reduced to retrieving their water from wells, springs and streams, some of which were deemed to be detrimental to health.

At a Fire Brigade Committee meeting on 13 September 1861, a report into the fire brigade was read out which informed the committee that two fires had occurred recently, and that the relevant insurance companies had been applied to for the expenses incurred by the brigade. It was also stated that the town's fire bell, which was situated on the police station wall, was cracked and needed replacing. After the brief report, the committee concluded that, following their discussions, the fire brigade would not be allowed any charges for refreshments when they attended fires, as the sum already paid them during fires (1s 6d for the first hour and 1s for any hour thereafter) was deemed to be sufficient compensation.

The town was presented with a new fire bell by Mr Arnold, agent for the Birmingham Fire Office, on 4 October 1861. The bell was affixed to the police station wall. Twenty years earlier, on 21 August 1841, another Mr Arnold had presented a cheque to the council for £6 19s 6d, toward the cost of a fire engine.

At this time, some three years after the formation of the town's fire brigade, there was already evidence of the council's concern about the costs incurred by the brigade, and the continued need for some insurance companies to be contacted for their share of those costs. The suggestion was made that perhaps it would be better for the council to organise a volunteer fire brigade with a paid superintendent, preferably from a metropolitan brigade, as was common in other towns. It was also said that one volunteer was better than 12 paid men; this, of course, referred simply to the cost of paying members of the fire brigade.

At a fire on 11 October 1861 in the Packet Hotel, the engine, firemen and 52 assistants required for the pumping of the fire engine handles all did good work. The committee made reference to the fact that the fire brigade had incurred costs of £19 8s 4d, and the monthly bill for the fire brigade was £5.

It was at this time, during a Section House Committee meeting, that it was recommended that the superintendent of police allow his off-duty men to assist the fire brigade once a month. The police would thereby become acquainted with the working of the engines and the fire escape ladder, which would, apart from making the men more efficient, save the council money. The council would be able to defer any costs paid to the firemen for inspecting and testing the fire appliances and equipment. At a meeting on 29 November 1861, it was resolved that the superintendent of police be made responsible for the fire escape ladders. He would ensure their safe custody and place them at strategic points around the town.

The council seemed to consider the fire brigade a costly luxury, so it was no surprise that when the superintendent of the fire brigade made a request for caps, coats and belts, it was deferred. A further discussion ensued, at which Councillor Rees informed the meeting that he had received a complaint that the fire brigade had not arrived promptly at a recent fire in Temple Street. Alderman Phillips replied to this that he had been at the fire, and he was sure that the fire brigade and engine had arrived within four minutes. With the assistance of civilians, the fire brigade had prevented the spread of the fire by extinguishing it smartly. Despite this vindication of the brigade by Alderman Phillips, the fire brigade was no more popular at later meetings, and a request for new clothing was deferred until the accounts of the fire brigade were properly audited.

Prior to this meeting, a letter from the superintendent of the fire brigade, Mr John Morgan, was read out to the committee, confirming his intention to resign. At the following month's meeting, on 10 January 1862, the appointment of Mr William Dyer as replacement superintendent was announced. A month later Superintendent Dyer had his first fire in charge. A passing constable saw smoke and flames issuing from a house occupied by a Mr George in the Strand, and although he immediately raised the alarm, the fire had devastating and tragic consequences. The fire brigade arrived promptly, and a copious supply of water was available, but the properties of Mr George and his neighbour Mr Owen were completely gutted. Tragically, Mr George's 11-year-old daughter, Selina, was pronounced dead at the scene.

The issue of the expense of the fire brigade would not go away. At a meeting of the Fire Brigade Committee, the mayor made a speech on the matter: 'Their fire brigade was getting a very expensive affair, and he believed the time was not far distant when they would be obliged to make some very important alterations therein. For his own part he thought if the

Board (the Local Board of Health) provided and paid a brigade, and brought the engines to the spot in times of fire, they should not be called upon to pay the expenses.'

This statement by the mayor was a direct reference to the insurance companies, who he thought should be contributing on all occasions when fire occurred on properties insured by them. Several councillors present held the same opinion as the mayor. Mr E.M. Richards had already voiced his belief that when the brigade was formed, it should be self-supporting, funded by the money from the various insurance companies.

On 11 April 1862 the Fire Brigade Committee met, and a decision was made that was the 'final nail in the Fire Brigade's coffin'. It was suggested that the superintendent of police become the superintendent of the fire brigade. The cost of running and maintaining the fire brigade at this time was some £584. The Clerk of the Council was instructed to contact other boroughs to find out about the organisation of their police fire brigades. The proposal was carried, and was to lead to the demise of the fire brigade as a separate body from the police.

At a meeting of the Swansea Local Board of Health on 6 June 1862, referring to the minutes of the previous meeting regarding the remodelling of the fire brigade, they recommended that the present members of the fire brigade be immediately given notice by the town clerk, discontinuing their services at the earliest time practicable. Once that notice had expired the brigade would be constituted as follows:

The Superintendent of the Police to be the future Superintendent of the Fire Brigade and to have management and care thereof, and the engines, at a salary of £1 5s 0d per calendar month, amounting to £15 0s 0d per annum.

Four members of the Police Force to be appointed by the Superintendent to act as firemen, and to keep the engines and hose clean and in a good state of repair, along with other equipment, for this they would receive 2s 6d per calendar month or £1 10s 0d per annum.

15 assistants on each practice day (with a remuneration of 1s 6d, practice days were to be implemented at one a quarter.) Which practice days shall take place once every quarter and to be employed at 1s.6d for each (amounting to £4 10s 0d per annum) practice day, no extra allowance would be made to the Superintendent or the four policemen for that practice day.

(The above was instituted on 4 July 1862)

Mr T. Evans was appointed chairman of the Fire Brigade Committee on 27 November 1863, and recommended the purchase of a reel and 100ft of canvas hose, at a cost of 10d a foot, £10 of which had recently been donated by the Sun Insurance Office. The committee was further informed that with the introduction of the town's new water supply, there was sufficient pressure in the mains to throw a jet of water to great heights without the aid of the fire engine.

With the purchase of a hand cart for the conveyance of the hose and other equipment to fires, there would be a reduced need for the hire of horses, and fewer people would be needed to assist in working and transporting the engines, thus reducing the cost to ratepayers. There had previously been the need to pay 50 or 60 men for conveying the engines to the Union Workhouse (better known as Mount Pleasant Hospital) on Mount Pleasant Hill.

The superintendent of the fire brigade, in his report to the Fire Brigades Committee on 6 May 1864, gave details of a fire at the factory of Mr Hopkins, Woollen Manufacturers, in Waterloo Street. The police station was notified at 2.55am, and the Norwich Union and Corporation fire engines, along with members of the fire brigade, were on the spot by 3.05am. The fire was extinguished by 6am. The estimated loss to Mr Hopkins was around £4,000 and he was insured with the Birmingham Fire Office. With material assistance rendered from bystanders, the expenses for 63 engine assistants amounted to £9 3s 9d. The sum was ordered to be paid, and the relevant insurance offices duly applied to for their share.

As Swansea returned to its days of a police fire brigade, a serious fire occurred at Down's furniture warehouse, in the High Street, on 14 July 1863. The alarm was raised by women who worked at the establishment. When the town's fire bell was rung the brigade responded. Smoke and flames were issuing from the upper windows, and the mains were tapped and the hose run out. Unlike in earlier years, there was a good and copious supply of water available, so much so, that due to the increased pressure in the town's mains, the engines were not required. At the following Fire Brigade Committee meeting, Mr Richards informed those present that the pressure in the town's mains on the afternoon of the fire was everything that could be desired, and it was hoped that on the completion of the works, the same supply and pressure would be available to all parts of the town, and would render the need for the fire engines to attend unnecessary.

The risks and hazards of Swansea's location as a seaport town were brought to the fore when, at 9.50pm on 15 August 1864, a serious fire broke out on the barque SS *Mysore* in the Phoenix dry dock. The fire brigade responded, bringing the Norwich Union and Birmingham fire engines to the scene. A good supply of water was available and the firemen commenced playing their jets on to the ship. As the fire spread into the ships stays and rigging, it seemed that the total destruction of the ship was inevitable, until PC James Olden, in an act of heroic bravery and without any thought for his own personal safety, ascended the rigging and extinguished the fire. He prevented the foremast from falling and stopped the fire from spreading further.

After hearing the chief constable's report into the

incident, the council agreed to reward PC Olden with the payment of one guinea. All the policemen who had attended the fire were commended for their exertions.

An inventory of the engine room in 1865 stated that the contents were as follows:

Norwich Union Pump: (with fittings stamped No.1)

2 standcocks, 2 lengths of suction and feed pipes

3 nozzle pipes, 2 spare nozzles

1 breaching piece with 2 outlets, 1 gooseneck

1 key and spoon (for turning on the water)

1 jemmy and keys, 2 x 6ft ladders

Corporation engine: (stamped No.2)

2 standcocks

3 lengths of suction, and feed pipes.

3 nozzle pipes and spare nozzle

Birmingham Office Engine: (stamped No.3)

3 suction pipes

1 nozzle and spare nozzle

3 keys

28 lengths of hose

2 tubes lined with zinc

4 and three quarter dozen iron buckets

2 long handled sweeping brushes

2 oil cans

1 feeder

1 turpentine can

1 near foot oil can

1 strong iron bar.

3 axes

1 steel stamp

1 screw axe

1 reel cart with canvas hose

Looking at the inventory, the Birmingham engine has a large array of equipment. It would seem that it was a much bigger contraption than the Norwich and Corporation engines.

Water now seemed to be abundantly available to fight fires in the town, unlike during the early years.

Councillors were keen to mention that fires in the town could be fought without recourse to the town's fire engines, because of the water system adopted by the council. Hydrants now produced a greater pressure than the fire engine. The advantages of the hydrant over the fire engine were made plain at a Council meeting on 10 February 1865, when the expenses incurred by the fire brigade were discussed. The report made reference to the recent fire at the docks, when the engines required 44 men to work the handles, at a cost of £64 14s 0d. The costs were far lower at fires where a hydrant was in use and the engine was not required. It was further noted that off-duty police who assisted should be paid the same as the civilians.

A constant thorn in the fire brigade's side was the collection of monies due from the various insurance companies after a fire. The matter was discussed again at a Fire Brigade Committee meeting on 14 April 1865. There were costs of £88 outstanding from the insurers. Mr Evans proposed that the relevant companies should be contacted immediately after a fire, when he believed they were more willing to pay, and not at a later date. He also suggested that insurance companies that refused to pay should be publicly named. At the following month's meeting the superintendent informed the committee that he had visited various insurance offices in London, to ascertain how they paid the fire brigade for expenses incurred at fires, and was informed that they were always willing to pay their pro rata share of the expenses.

The Fire Brigade Committee met again on 23 February 1866. On the agenda was the possible increase of the fire brigade by two, making the number up to 12, and the provision of new uniforms. The superintendent recommended the permanent increase in manpower, at a cost of 5s extra per week. This was passed by the committee and the tenders for the uniforms were duly applied for.

Chapter Two

Tragedy Strikes

All fires are tragedies, none more so than when they are accompanied by the loss of life. In the early hours of Thursday 10 May 1866, Swansea encountered its worst fire to date, with the loss of eight lives. The fire occurred in a drapers shop, owned by Mr H.D. Johns, of 2 Temple Street.

PC Owen John, aged 21, had commenced his shift at 9pm that evening and was the first to discover the fire. He was in Temple Street searching for a brooch which had been reported lost. He heard a crackling noise like that of a fire, and on further investigation discovered, by looking through the window shutters, that the rear of the shop premises at No.2 was ablaze. He immediately ran to the nearby police station in Temple Street and informed Inspector Ball. Together they returned to the scene and proceeded to hammer on the doors and windows in the hope of alerting the inmates.

This noise and commotion disturbed the neighbours, and Mr Clayton, a confectioner, ran across to the shop to offer assistance. He peered through the shop's letter box, further confirming that the rear of the shop was ablaze. Stones and pieces of coal were being thrown at the upstairs windows with the hope of alerting those inside. This had the desired effect, and two people came to the second-floor window. The pair were thought to be female, and PC John shouted for them to remain at the window while he ran for the escape ladder, which was stored at the castle yard. On reaching the yard, PC John found that the castle gate was locked so he was unable to bring out the ladder. Valuable time was lost as he returned to the police station to locate the key. Unable to find it, he returned to the castle yard with an iron bar and accompanied by another constable and several civilians. They broke the chain from the gate and were then able to lower the ladder and return to the fire. The escape ladder was placed against the upper window of the second storey, and Inspector Ball immediately ascended, followed by PC John. There were as yet no flames at the front of the house, only smoke. Below, the street was thronged with onlookers. In a short space of time Inspector Ball was handed Mr Johns's youngest child Nellie, aged two and a half, who he passed to the waiting PC John. This was followed by the exit of Miss Annie Wooton, an assistant employed by Mr Johns. Both were brought down the ladder to safety. The police officers remained aloft, and Inspector Ball stood on the sill calling for those in the house to come to him. The building was now belching smoke, and flames had appeared at the upper windows.

The hose was carried up the escape ladder and played into the upper rooms, which were now well alight. The onlookers voiced their anxieties – some

The memorial erected by public subscription to the eight people who lost their lives at John's draper's shop, Temple Street, Swansea, on 10 May 1866. (Author's collection)

thought that all the people inside must be safe, but nothing could be further from the truth. The flames began to issue from every opening, including the window where the escape ladder was positioned. Even though there was no lack of water, the jets from the hoses had little effect against the ferocity of the flames.

While Inspector Ball and PC Owen John had been procuring the escape ladder and rescuing the child and assistant, Inspector Crockford had been instrumental in bringing out the fire engine and equipment. The standpipes were set into the fire plugs, and the hose was played on the front of the house in Temple Street. At the rear of the premises, which could be accessed from a lane, the fire was at its worst. Before Inspector Crockford and other members of the brigade arrived on the scene, two men, Henry Richards of Seabeach Terrace and Janus Evans of Recorder Street, had left their place of work at the South Dock when they heard the fire bell, and proceeded to the

scene of the fire. In the back lane the were confronted by two women and Edwin Poole of Goat Street, who took them to the rear of the shop hoping that they would be able to help rescue those inside. Although the men successfully entered the shop, the flames had taken too firm a hold. Parts of the internal structure collapsed around them, and their only option was to retreat, in the firm belief that no one could be saved from the flames.

The fire continued for some three hours or more, and resulted in the total destruction of premises. Next day all that was left was the gruesome task of recovering the burnt remains of the eight persons who perished.

Following the inquest into the Temple Street fire, the jury recommended that these representations be appended:

1. That in future, the escape in the town should be so placed that it may be used by the public or the Police, that a second escape should be provided and a catch sheet attached to each as well as a small crow bar and speaking trumpet.
2. That the 'fire bell' has been and is liable to be mistaken for other bells in frequent use in the town and therefore a special town bell should be substituted.
3. That every exertion was used by the members of the Police Force and that a water supply was ample.
4. Lastly that Inspector Ball performed his duties to the satisfaction of the jury.

The expenses of the fire brigade at the recent fire amounted to £18 19s 0d. These were allowed and the superintendent was directed to apply immediately to the insurance offices for the repayment of their share.

A letter of appreciation from a Mr Evan Evans, a neighbour at an adjoining property, was received by the council. It reads:

Dear Sir,

Under a sense of deep obligation to yourself and every member of the Police Force on duty in Temple Street on the unfortunate morning of Thursday last, I beg to forward you a cheque for £10 for distribution among your men, not for a moment deeming such a sum anything like sufficient reward for their valuable services in saving my property from utter destruction, (which I can attribute to your prompt and judicious arrangements and to the zeal and activity displayed by your men in carrying them out) but merely as a mark of my gratitude and appreciation of you and their conduct.

The cheque presented was distributed amongst the members who attended the fire accordingly:

Superintendent of the fire brigade, Chief
    Constable Allison   £2
Inspectors Crockford and Ball, and Constable
    Olden   10s each.
Sergeants Williams and Holland, Constables
    Barnett, John and Bowden   5s each.

This shows a discrepancy, and one can only assume that this was distributed to other members present.

An inspector of fire engines had also attended the fire, and he was heard to comment on the agility of Inspector Crockford and Constable Olden in ascending the fire escape. He said he thought 'they were members of the London Brigade.'

The superintendent of the fire brigade, Chief Constable Allison, recommended to the Local Board of Health Meeting on 18 May 1866, that a new fire escape ladder be purchased for the use of the fire brigade, at a cost not exceeding £45. The super-intendent would undertake to place it in an accessible position in the town. The proposal was approved, and on 22 June a new fire escape ladder arrived from Henry Marriott of Preston. The cost was £45, plus a carriage charge of £1 1s 11d.

At a meeting on 29 June 1866, the Fire Brigade Committee was informed that a new cast steel bell had been ordered at a cost of £11 10s 0d, which weighed 216lb. Although the print of the estimate for the bell is clear, I cannot believe that this is other than a misprint of 216lb, as a fire bell from the Goat Street Station (1884-1905) that I have in my possession weighs only 40lbs.

Some eleven years later, on 24 August 1877, a monument was erected at the Danygraig Cemetery. It was paid for by public subscription. The report at the time stated that a

…substantial monument of Forest of Dean stone has been erected in Swansea Cemetery, on the grave of Mr H.D. Johns, draper, and those who perished in the calamitous fire that took place at No.2 Temple Street, in 1866. The design is an obelisk supported by a die or base, resting on a plinth and platform 3ft square and surrounded by an iron railing, the whole, being about 12ft high, the inscriptions are arranged on the east side of the obelisk, and on three faces of the obelisk.

This monument
by public
subscription
to the memory of
the eight persons
who perished
in the
destructive fire
that took place at
Mr H.D. John's
Drapery
establishment
at No.2 Temple Street
Swansea.
on 10 day of May
1866.

Henry David John
Son of Henry and Elizabeth John
of
Newport, Monmouthshire
aged 38 years

Louisa John
Wife of the above
aged 27 years

Hettie John
Daughter of the above
aged four years
Luke X11 2,3,4,5.
On the north face of the base is inscribed:
Margaret Esther Davies
Daughter of
Thomas and Elizabeth Davies
of
Newport, Pembrokeshire
Aged 21 years

Sarah Deacon
of
Shropshire
Aged 19 years

Fanny Smith
of
Llanelly
Aged 19 years
Assistants
James 1V 14
On the east face of the base is inscribed:
Catherine Howells
of
Llansamlet
Aged 45 years

Annie Edwards
of
Swansea
Aged 16 years
Servants
Proverbs XXV11 1

(Temple Street was approximately situated between

the present David Evans store and Castle Gardens, and linked Castle Street and Goat Street. The monument to the Temple Street fire victims can be seen in the present-day photograph.)

An accident involving the recently-purchased fire escape occurred on 14 September 1866. During an exercise, a strong gust of wind caught the canvas rescue sheet of the escape, tipping it over. Unfortunately, the young daughter of a nearby chemist was passing, and the upper part of the ladder struck her, inflicting a severe scalp wound. The committee agreed to pay Mr Williams's medicine bill, but this was not the end of the matter. On 2 April 1867 the sum of £20 was agreed by the council in lieu of any claim brought by Mr Williams, but this sum must have been rejected, as at a further meeting on 4 June 1867, the Town Clerk informed the committee that a letter had been received from Mr Williams, claiming damages of £100. It was then recommended that the settlement for any claim against the Local Board of Health be left entirely for the attention of the Town Clerk. There is no record of a settlement of the claim made by Mr Williams.

The skill and resolve of Inspector Crockford as a fireman was tested again on 25 April 1867, when a fire broke out on the premises of Colpoy's, photographer and toy dealer, immediately under the castle clock. The fire, which occurred in the early hours of Saturday morning, broke out on the second floor. As the police station was close by, prompt assistance was at hand. Four people had to be rescued by the fire escape ladder, which at the time was under the supervision of Inspector Crockford and the chief constable.

Swansea was becoming well used to dealing with serious fires. In the early hours of 2 October 1867, Bryn y Mor House, the residence of Mr Robert Eaton Esq., was reported to be on fire. Mrs Eaton, who had thought she had heard intruders, investigated and she smelled burning. She immediately woke everyone in the house and they made their escape. The alarm bell at the rear of the house was rung to summon assistance. On hearing the bell, Police Constable Cowan, who was stationed at Sketty, hurried to investigate. On arrival at the house he observed that the fire had already taken a firm hold, and proceeded to alert the fire brigade.

A brisk westerly breeze was blowing which, coupled with the elevated location of the house, and the fact that it was predominately of timber construction, meant that the flames spread at an alarmingly rapid pace. Two hose carts and the engine were in attendance, and a standpipe was affixed into the main opposite the entrance. Jets were played on the building, but the whole of the upper storey and the west side of the roof were ablaze. Even with a plentiful supply of water, the jets seemed to be having little effect on the flames, so most of the firemen's efforts were concentrated on saving the undamaged contents. Some good was done, and some valuable oil paintings and furniture were saved. The fire was finally extinguished at 8am, at which point the extent of the damage could be properly assessed.

The chief constable, who had been in attendance throughout, made a report to the Fire Brigade Committee, in which he was to replied to a criticism made of fire brigade, that there had been a delay in their response to the alarm. His report concluded that from the time of the message being received at the police station, some 18 minutes had elapsed before the fire brigade arrived at the scene. There was conflicting evidence about the cause of the delay, but it seemed that two civilians, who had promised to alert the fire brigade, neglected to do so.

The mayor defended the fire brigade, remarking that he had been at the scene of the fire, and was of the opinion that the fire brigade had behaved themselves in an exemplary fashion. They had even risked their personal safety when retrieving valuable contents from the flames, and Sergeant Holland and Constable Morris (20) deserved special praise for their efforts.

Although Morriston was approximately four miles from Swansea, it was within the borough boundaries. At a Town Council meeting on 18 February 1869, Mr Richard Hughes inquired whether steps had been taken to provide the Morriston district with its own police station. The chief constable replied that a fire reel and hose had been provided for the district of Morriston, but because there was no suitable place to store them, they were still at Swansea police station. Once a police station was erected at Morriston, they would be transferred for use in an emergency.

Further concern about Morriston's vulnerability to an outbreak of fire arose when it was reported that in May of that year the supply from the Lliw Reservoir would be turned off every night from 6pm to 6am, due to a serious leak in the mains.

On 3 February 1871, the barque *Midsummer* from Sunderland, which was in dock in Swansea, caught fire. PC John Thomas, who was on duty near the South Dock, saw smoke issuing from the cabin of the vessel. He immediately went on board, and found that a cabin was ablaze. He dispatched a messenger to alarm the fire brigade, and having rung the ship's bell, which brought no response, he tried to extinguish the blaze with buckets of water. When the fire brigade arrived with the requisite appliances, the cabin and the quarter deck were completely enveloped in flames. The firemen commenced operations, and thanks to a copious supply of water were able to extinguish the fire. Damage was sustained by the ship's sails, ropes, mizzen mast and quarter deck, as well as an adjacent vessel.

The transferring of the Temple Street police station to the Town Hall in Somerset Place, near the dock area of the town, was on the agenda for a Town Council meeting in April 1872. The committee were divided, and the main issue was the new, inconvenient location of the town's fire engines and equipment and the extra distance involved in transporting the engines to the town centre. Additionally, when the fire bell at Temple Street was rung it could be heard all over town, but this would not be the case if it were transferred to the Town Hall. A protracted discussion resulted in the proposal to relocate being approved. The mayor and other councillors were appointed to make the necessary arrangements.

Chapter Three

Proposed New Stations

The long-awaited purpose-built police fire station at Morriston became a reality when, on 14 June 1872, land was acquired from the Duke of Beaufort for the sum of 50 guineas. The plot in question was situated at the junction of Martin Street and Banwell Street. Morriston also required a market, and some monies had already been collected for funding the project. The council agreed to take over these monies, and provide a police fire brigade station with a reading room (library) and a market incorporated in the design.

Meanwhile, Swansea Town Council was involved in further discussions about the relocation of the Temple Street police station. Estimates had even been produced for the purchase and building of a new station in the High Street. The costs would amount to:

Building a lock-up etc. in the High Street
£765 0s 0d
Alterations to the cells and Quay Dues Offices
£130 0s 0d
Purchase of the freehold site in the High Street
£620.0s 0d
Total £1,515.0s 0d

The estimated income from letting the present police station in Temple Street was £160 per annum. To alter the present station in Temple Street would cost £580, and renting part of the adjoining premises for an extension to the Court would cost £150 per annum. The council saw that the borough stood to make large savings, and voted to adopt the scheme.

The council surveyor, Mr Cousens, had prepared two plans, with estimates, for the erection of a police station in the High Street, one on the site of No.61, and the other on the site of Nos 79 and 80, at the south-east corner of Tontine Street. The committee recommended that they proceed with the building of a new police fire brigade station on the latter site. (The building was the old Fred Ley, Fruiterer's, until it burnt down in 1980.)

At a further meeting of the Town Council in November 1872, it was decided to merge the Fire Brigade Committee with the Watch Committee. The new committee would comprise the mayor and Messrs J. Glassbrook, P. Rogers, Phillips, J. Rogers, Rees, Richards, T. Glassbrook, Glover, Jenkins, Harry and Hughes. It was then reported that the police court in Temple Street would cease to be used as such, and would shortly be sold or let.

The ensuing closure of the Temple Street station prompted the burgesses and ratepayers of the town to produce a signed testimonial, which claimed that as the town's population was increasing rapidly, it would better if the police fire brigade station remained in Temple Street. The document was presented to the mayor and Mr Thomas Ford Esq. on 20 December 1872, and also stated that the central position of the well-constructed building, suitably adapted for the purpose of which it was built, coupled with the convenience of the fire alarm bell, fire escape ladder and other appliances, meant that the council should reconsider its recommendation.

This demonstration of public concern about the removal of the Temple Street station was to no avail, as on 4 April 1873, the council accepted the tender of Mr John Buse, Saddler & Co. of Oxford Street, for a 75-year lease on the property at a cost of £150 per annum.

In the early hours of Sunday morning on 30 May 1873, a fire was discovered by Constables Williams and Thompson. They saw smoke issuing from the shutters of Mr Thomas Phillips's grocers shop in Oxford Street, and ran to the police station to raise the alarm. The Inspector sent for the turncock and rang the fire bell. The chief constable and members of the fire brigade responded, only to find on their arrival at the scene that the town's main was turned off at night. Although a hydrant was fixed within ten minutes and the mains turned on, the supply could only be described as a dribble. The Oxford Street main had not been renewed for many years and corrosion had greatly reduced its internal dimensions. This caused a further delay, as the firemen obtained a supply from the Goat Street and College Street mains, running their hoses to the scene of the fire in Oxford Street.

By this time a delay of 45 minutes had occurred, and the fire had obtained such a hold that it was rapidly spreading to the adjoining premises. Mr Phillips's shop was beyond saving, and the firefighters could only battle to save the neighbouring buildings. When the fire was finally extinguished at 7.30am, all that remained was a mass of smouldering ruins, and a loss of several thousand pounds.

The Oxford Street fire added to the growing public concern about the closure of the Temple Street station. A query in the local press was asked: 'Another subject for consideration is, how, with a divided Police Station, the Superintendent of Police and Officers being kept in High Street, fire engines etc., kept in another, fire bell, no one knows where, how can they turn out at short notice with such divided arrangements?'

The constant barrage of letters in the local press, as well as further signatures to the document opposing the closure of the Temple Street station, led the mayor, following a meeting with a deputation, to remark that his opinion on the matter had changed. He now believed that with the town growing so rapidly (words that echoed those of a ratepayer in the press), more police accommodation would be required. The fate of the central Temple Street station premises, should therefore be re-thought. Although the matter was already out of the council's hands, the mayor recommended that the deputation should meet with Mr Buse. Mr Buse replied that he had already speculated on the premises and, with its increased revenue, the council would profit by way of the rates.

A letter in agreement with the council's policy was printed in the local press, in which the writer pointed out that the location of the police or fire brigade station did not guarantee safety or better protection for the nearby properties. Some years previously a house within yards of the fire brigade station had been completely consumed with the loss of eight lives (the Temple Street fire at Mr H.D. Johns).

The continuation of the debate brought about an address from the chief constable at a Town Council meeting on 15 August 1873. He and his men were occupying premises at the Town Hall, and fire appliances were kept at the Town Hall and at the new High Street Station. The chief constable believed that a further station, situated at the west end of the town, would complete the arrangements for providing fire cover for the whole town.

Morriston police fire brigade station pictured when it was in use, and how it looks today. (Author's collection and Edwin Brimble)

The mayor, in complete contrast to his previous statement to the deputation, fully endorsed the chief constable's recommendations. He concluded that they should be adopted, as it would benefit the town more than retaining the old station.

In the meantime, tenders had been received from various builders, and the committee decided that the tender from Mr Thos. White, a builder of Swansea, be accepted for the erection of a Market Hall and police station at Morriston. This was the lowest tender, and was for £2,750 for the police station and £739 for the market.

With regard to the location of the police fire brigade stations, none could have been more appropriately positioned than the one at the Town Hall in East Burrows when, at between 5am and 6am on 27 November 1873, a serious fire broke out on the premises of Mr J.W. Pockett. A man named Lewis heard an explosion which shook the whole area. He then observed smoke issuing from Pockett's Wharf, and evidence of flames within. He instantly raised the alarm at the nearby police station in the Town Hall. Fortunately, the shift was just changing and the whole of the police force was present, including the officers that formed the fire brigade. No time was lost in moving all the available engines and equipment to the scene, along with a large number of harbour workmen.

The large body of men worked with vigour, energy and willingness, which did them great credit. However, even with an abundant supply of water from the mains, their efforts were futile. The fire had gained such a hold on the premises that all the contents, including groceries, palm oil, raisins and petroleum were beyond saving. The inflammable nature of the materials stored meant that the fire burned furiously, defying the volumes of water which were thrown upon it. The flames shot up into the air, illuminating the whole of the adjacent district, and at times a can of benzoline would explode with a roar like a canon. The fire eventually burned itself out, leaving only a mass of smouldering ruins. How the fire started was unknown, but the damage was believed to run to several thousands of pounds.

On 2 January 1874, the borough force saw the opening of the High Street police fire brigade station. The new station was a relief to the eye, with its dressed stone front, and was a stark comparison to the many tumbledown structures of the district. The town now had three strategically-located stations: the one in Lower Oxford Street (at the rear of the old Eddershaws shop in St Helen's Road), which would serve the St Helen's and Sandfields districts, the new station in the High Street, and the Town Hall station for the shipping and docks area, which also acted as the town's police headquarters.

The mistake of relying on the town's main for supplying water for firefighting was once more brought to the fore on the night of 31 July 1874. A telegraphic message was sent to the High Street station, informing the police that a fire had broken out at the Hafod Steel Works, and their immediate assistance was required. The fire brigade, who unfortunately were under strength because some constables had not yet returned from the police annual outing, arrived on the scene. They saw that the fire had taken a firm hold on the building, and attempted to access the works hydrants for a supply. However, the brigade's hose would not fit onto the works hydrant, which led to a delay in getting the hose to play on the flames. This in turn increased the amount of damage which was eventually caused by the fire.

The districts of Hafod and Landore saw many fires because of the concentration of factories in those areas. One fire occurred on the night of 29 October 1874, which resulted in the total destruction of the Landore railway station. A constable who was stationed in the area saw smoke issuing from the booking office, and after a further investigation he raised the alarm. The Swansea fire brigade were telegraphed for, and neighbouring trucks and quantities of goods were removed in the interval before they arrived. The station was constructed mainly of wood, which caused the flames to spread rapidly, and by the time the Swansea brigade arrived, under the command of the chief constable, Mr Allison, the station was 'a large edifice on the conspicuous site being a brilliant, but startling beacon to the lower portion of the Swansea Vale.'

Although a plentiful supply of water was available from the nearby mains, as well as from the station's tanks, the building was completely destroyed. The fire was caused by the constant depositing of hot cinders and ashes on a nearby tip. Beneath the tip, the ground was of a partial peat compound and this, along with the station's main wooden supports, which had been set well into the ground, eventually ignited.

Despite the nearness of the Town Hall station to a fire at Austen's Boat and Block Works, at the South Dock, the fire brigade encountered further delays in obtaining water. Although the turncock was present, the delay was attributed to the complex nature of the town's water supplies. Opening and closing various valves to redirect the water took time. As in previous incidents, the *Cambrian* published a letter to the editor: 'Why our fire engines are not overhauled monthly, as here to fore, had the engines used on Wednesday night been in a proper working order, a supply of water could have been brought to play on the fire, at least 15 minutes sooner, than the water was had from the mains.' The letter was signed by 'one who came with the engine.'

This was alluded to at a Watch Committee meeting, when the chief constable's report recommended that the police should be instructed in the operations of the turncock. There were currently only two turncocks, and to have police trained to carry out their tasks would prevent further delays in obtaining a water supply at fires. The chief constable further stated that the Swansea stations, along with the Morriston branch, be connected by telegraph. Communication between the stations would be very helpful at outbreaks of fire occurred. The committee agreed the proposals.

The need for a policy on water supply was demonstrated again on 12 August 1875. A serious fire broke out in the shop of Mr Roberts, Draper, in Oxford Street. The fire was discovered at about 9.30pm on Wednesday, and the shutters were immediately removed and goods brought out from the premises. Unfortunately this action vented the fire, and soon flames burst through the windows and doors and projected across the pavement. The fire

brigade, who arrived on the scene in 10–15 minutes, were under the command of the chief constable and accompanied by a number of the borough police force. For some inconceivable reason the water had been turned off at the mains, and yet again there was a delay in locating the turncock and getting the water turned on. The heroics of the firemen were once again noteworthy, as with no regard for their personal safety they manned the hoses from the various ladders, projecting their jets into the flames. The fire, which was attended by the usual hoards of onlookers, continued for some hours and resulted in the total destruction of the premises.

Another spectacular fire in Swansea took place in the early hours of Saturday 17 November 1875. At about 4am, information was received by the police relating to an outbreak of fire at the large premises of Messrs Johnson and Burgess, ship chandlers, on the Strand. Sergeant Flynn, in charge at the Town Hall, and Inspector Ball, in charge of the High Street detachment, hastened to the scene with all their available constables and the hoses and standpipes. Eventually, the whole of the fire brigade and the police force was in attendance. Before jets of water could be trained on the flames, the officers were confronted with the usual problem of obtaining water from the mains. After digging out the fire plug at the hydrant opposite the shop of Mr Martin, the jeweller in Wind Street, there was no water available, and the same problem was found at the hydrant in Quay Parade. Eventually a good supply was obtained from the hydrant on the Strand at the rear of the Mackworth Hotel. (At this time the Mackworth Hotel was situated on the site of the Wind Street post office, now the 'The Square'.) Water was sought from five hydrants, but could only be drawn from three. Given the proximity of this fire and others to the docks, where there was an abundant supply of water, we can only assume that there were still difficulties with the condition of or operating of the engines.

The fire at Messrs Johnson and Burgess assumed

large dimensions when, at around 5am, the roof collapsed. The flames issued forth from all windows, and the highly inflammable stock, including oil and turpentine, ignited. The fire was fanned by a strong, gale force wind, and continued to burn unabated as the fire brigade concentrated its efforts on saving the adjacent buildings. After the fire it was thought that the only reason that the fire never extended to the whole block was due to the energetic efforts of the fire brigade.

Although the origin of the fire was unknown, the costs incurred by the total destruction of the premises and stock were believed to be around £8,000–£9,000.

Mr Cousens, whose property abutted the scene of the fire, wrote in the *Cambrian* following the fire:

> …that the difficulty for the fire brigade in obtaining water from the mains, was due to the hydrants being positioned in the middle of a muddy street, which allowed them to be choked up with stones and earth, therefore, when required at a fire, some long delays were incurred in locating them.

He further commented on the praiseworthy efforts of the fire brigade, with particular mention of police officers Flynn, Gardner and Johnson.

A fire at Mr Hache's carpenter's shop, in Crole Street off Walter Road, on 12 May 1876, had serious consequences for Inspector Ball. He was standing near a high wall when he was struck on the head by falling masonry, which knocked him to the ground. While lying on the ground in shock he was showered by falling debris from a nearby 20ft wall. His thigh was fractured and he was conveyed to the Swansea Hospital.

At a meeting in December 1876, a report was read out stating that it had been brought to the attention of the committee that Inspector Ball was permanently disabled after his accident he incurred at the fire, and was unable to fulfil his duties within the force. It was recommended that he be given a superannuation allowance of 28s a week, with a further 14s a week as the collector for samples for the public analysis department under Head Constable Allison. It was further resolved that the head constable should present Inspector Ball with a badge for distinguished bravery in the saving of life or property, to be worn on the arm.

Chapter Four

Captain Isaac Colquhoun

The Watch Committee meeting on 12 October 1877 discussed disclosed irregularities in the accounts of the borough police force. Although he was not directly involved, the head constable, Mr Allison had resigned. This revelation fuelled arguments, as did the question of the duties and salary of the head constable. He had received: as head constable of police, £300 per annum, as inspector of weights and measures, £25 per annum, as inspector of contagious diseases (animals), £10 per annum, allowance for clothing, £10, for the keep of a horse, £60 per annum, as chief of the fire brigade, £15 per annum – a total of £420 per annum. The arguments continued and some people published their own interpretation of what the head constable's salary and responsibilities should be in the local press. One such letter recommended that the overall responsibility and command of the fire brigade rest with an inspector, whose pay would reflect the responsibility.

A month later an advert appeared for the post of superintendent of the borough police force, at a salary of £300 per annum, with £10 for clothing and a further £15 for being superintendent of the fire brigade. After the breakdown of the head constable's salary, some of his responsibilities and expenses had either been rescinded or transferred to other individuals.

Six candidates appeared before the Watch Committee in November 1877 for the post of head constable. After some lengthy interviews, the press and burgesses were informed that the successful candidate and new head constable for Swansea was Captain Isaac Colquhoun.

Captain Isaac Colquhoun had formerly been a captain in the 17th Regiment of Foot, and had served eight years in the Carmarthenshire Constabulary. He was considered to be a gentleman of fine bearing and character, as well as an excellent horseman. During his 35 years as head constable of the borough force he would gain the affection and confidence of the townspeople, and add to the dignity, prestige and reputation of the town's fire brigade. Prior to his inception as head constable and superintendent of the fire brigade, the brigade was composed of volunteers, chiefly drawn from the artisan classes: plumbers, joiners, masons, and the like. These volunteers, who augmented the police and fire services, lived in all parts of the town and were collected by on-duty policemen when required. The brigade used the old manual appliances, which were fed from the street mains (fire plugs). As no hydrants had reasonable pressure, the engines required many men to operate them, as many as 22 at a time. They needed frequent breaks from the arduous work.

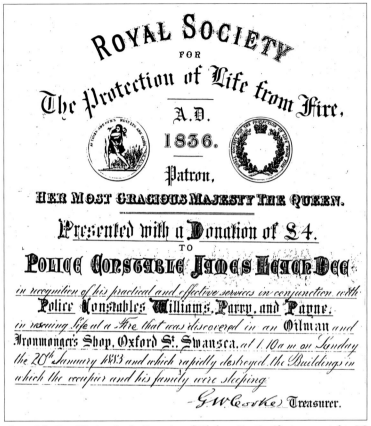

ROYAL SOCIETY

FOR

The Protection of Life from Fire,

A.D.

1836.

Patron,

HER MOST GRACIOUS MAJESTY THE QUEEN.

Presented with a Donation of $4.

TO

POLICE CONSTABLE James Leach Dee

in recognition of his practical and effective services in conjunction with
POLICE Constables Williams, Parry, *and* Payne,
in rescuing life at a Fire that was discovered in an OILMAN *and*
IRONMONGER'S Shop, Oxford St. Swansea, *at 1.10 a.m. on Sunday*
the 20th January 1883 and which rapidly destroyed the Buildings in
which the occupier and his family were sleeping.

— *G. W. Cooke* Treasurer.

Copy of the Royal Society for the Protection of Life from Fire Certificate, presented to PC James Leach Dee, following his rescues at the Oxford Street fire on 20 January 1883. (Swansea Archives, the Guildhall)

Captain Colquhoun's baptism as superintendent of the fire brigade came in January 1878 when he, along with Inspectors Holland, Jones, Williams and Staddon and 25 constables, attended a serious fire at the old Landore Steel Works.

The St Thomas Police Station was to be one of Captain Colquhoun's first targets for attention. It was decided that a new premises was required and should be found. A hose and reel could be stored there in case of fire in the district.

Police bravery was the next topic for discussion. At a fire in Richardson Street on 5 April 1878, constables Lewis (30) and Bowman (29) helped rescue two females and two children. The head constable, who had been in attendance throughout the fire, arranged for their bravery to be publicly recognised at a council meeting. The mayor donned his official robes and chain of office to attend a specially convened presentation at the police court in July, when the two constables, along with a civilian named David Davies, were presented with a record of their bravery, a testimonial written on vellum.

After nearly a year in office, at a meeting in October 1878, Captain Colquhoun requested an increase in the force's numbers, offering Cardiff as a comparison. A census in 1877 recorded the population of Cardiff as 60,536, and that of Swansea as 51,702, a difference of 8,835. There were 90 police in Cardiff, and two engineers for the fire brigade. Swansea's police ought, given these figures, to number 64 in total. The report was discussed and the council agreed to an increase of six men. The number of constables in the fire brigade would increase from

Under Captain Colquhoun the whole situation would change.

Although new in office, Captain Colquhoun led by example and exerted constant pressure on the authorities for change, dramatic and radical change of the town's fire services. He advocated the building of new stations, the supply of hydrants for firefighting purposes and the linking of stations by telephone to replace the old ABC telegraph system. This would put every member of the fire brigade into ready communication with a central authority. In achieving his aims, Colquhoun won for Swansea the honour of being one of the very first towns to recognise the value of the telephone as an aid, not only to the fire brigade, but also in police work.

14 to 20, and they would be paid 1s a week.

Captain Colquhoun continued to make demands of the council. On 7 January 1880, during his monthly report, he recommended that a more central police fire brigade station be considered, which would also act as a fire brigade headquarters. Given the difficulties encountered by the council when moving the Temple Street station to the High Street in 1874, his recommendation was deferred for debate at a future meeting. The council questioned the head constable about delays at a recent fire at the Landore Steel Works.

The Albert Medal presented to PC Dee.

The head constable explained that when the fire brigade arrived they were unable to locate the valve to turn on the water supply. Of 30 works in the district, not one made provision for the extinguishing of fires. He proposed that to alleviate the delays hydrants should be inserted every 300 yards. The fire brigade should be provided with horses for the engines, and the Landore police station, if retained, should be renovated and have a turncock on duty.

In February 1880, there was another major fire in Swansea. Without the alertness of some neighbours, and the heroic efforts of Constable Bowman, it would probably have resulted in the loss of lives. The fire, which occurred at the premises of Mr Jenkin Jones, drapers, in Castle Street, was discovered by a neighbour, who immediately raised the alarm. The lower floors were well alight, and the Jones family, along with their two assistants, were seen at the upper windows. With a ladder procured by one of the neighbours, PC Bowman ascended, entered the room and began to pass the occupants to Mr John Davies,

first the children, then the others. Yet again there was a delay in obtaining a water supply, and some 20 minutes elapsed before a good supply was available. By this time the fire had spread to the upper floors, and the firemen could only save the adjoining properties.

The Castle Street fire added weight to Captain Colquhoun's recommendations about the need for a more central police fire brigade station. Letters to the *Cambrian* newspaper recommenced, and included views on the delay in obtaining a water supply, the fact that the fire brigade had been left wanting and the idea that the town should re-consider its position on establishing a volunteer fire brigade. Comparisons were made with towns such as Colchester and Hitchin. These suggestions fell on deaf ears. The council had already been down that avenue and returned to a police fire brigade.

However, some moves were made to act on the suggestions of the townspeople. At a meeting on 3 March 1880, it was proposed that the head constable be authorised to engage 20 men, living in the locality of the different police stations, to act as volunteer firemen. They would be paid 10s a year for their services, and their names and addresses would be kept at the station.

The head constable's most radical statement about the fire brigade to date was made at a council meeting on 15 July 1880. He opened his report by stating that the present system adopted by the fire brigade was 'very bad' and in his view had to change. He offered two alternatives for the re-organisation of the fire brigade. Under the current system, the three stations were approximately three-quarters of a mile apart. In the event of a fire, all the constables on duty in the

The County Borough of Swansea fire brigade outside the old Guildhall, Somerset Place, in 1888. (Swansea fire brigade)

streets would leave their beats, which left areas of the town unprotected. If beat officers did not hear the alarm there would be insufficient numbers of men to attend the fire. Fire appliances were scattered about the town, and the escape ladder, due to insufficient personnel, often did not get taken to the scene of a fire, particularly after 3am when there were only six or seven constables on duty. During a fire, the High Street police station was left in charge of a person who did not belong to the force, which was not right, especially when the cells were occupied. Also there was no distinction made between the functions of the police or firemen. Policemen ought to keep back the crowds and protect the property from plunder, while firemen ought to extinguish the flames. Finally, much damage was done by water in the hands of those

unskilled policemen who were not properly trained as firemen.

The head constable's first alternative to the present system proposed that, in the event of the council not providing a larger station in the centre of the town, all the fire brigade appliances should be centralised at the High Street police fire brigade station. All fire brigade personnel should also be stationed there. More men would be available in the event of a fire, as all trained firemen would be put on to beats near that station. This would ensure that there were always trained personnel attending fires, and the station would be left in charge of a constable. If all the fire appliances were stationed at the High Street Station, there would be fewer constables required at the other stations. This would also alleviate damage to police uniforms, when police had to act as firemen.

The second alternative proposed that a new central police fire brigade station be erected, and that station houses be rented near the section house in Lower Oxford Street. These would be used by the firemen and a turncock, and would be fitted with alarm bells. Captain Colquhoun stressed that he strongly recommended the housing of a turncock, as a complete knowledge of re-routing of the water supply was required at fires. The council, in reply to this report, proposed that the recommendations made by the head constable be given due consideration by the committee.

A Merryweather 'Greenwich Gem' steam fire engine of the 1890s. This particular steamer is currently owned by the South Wales Fire Service, and is believed to be the one purchased by the Briton Ferry fire brigade in 1892. (Author's collection)

The mayor, in a statement following the visit and inspection of the borough police and fire brigade, said that although he had not personally attended the inspection made by Captain Elgee, the Government's Inspector of Constabularies, he had been informed of it by Councillor Daniel Jones. Captain Elgee had stated in his report that the High Street police and fire brigade station, was only fit to be a branch station, as all the cells had been badly constructed. Those at the Guildhall police station were only fit for prisoners awaiting trial. The report went on to criticise the present system. The inspector considered that such a small force ought not to be used as a fire brigade. If they were to fight fires they should at least be supplied with the relevant clothing. The inspector found the offices and stations to be worse than any he had seen in the south and north of England, or in South Wales. He recommended that a central police fire brigade station with 12 cells be provided. The similarity between the inspector's report and the recommendations put forward by Captain Colquhoun were obvious, and the question of whether they had colluded was raised.

The issue of delays and difficulties experienced with the water supply at fires was again brought to the fore after a fire at the Brush Manufactory of Lewis and Son, in Oxford Street. The head constable was asked to explain the problems, and he reported that the hose and reel had been taken to the fire within four minutes, and the 30-minute delay was the result of the turncock being away from home, and the water being turned off. During that time, however, the new Sinclair chemical extinguisher had been brought to the scene and used to some effect. Councillor Chapman asked what precautions the head constable had taken to ensure that a delay did not occur in the future.

To this the head constable replied that the fire brigade would never be worked satisfactorily with the present arrangements. He had reported on the subject and suggested another system, but nothing had been done. The subject was then dropped. This was some two years after Captain Colquhoun had made his initial recommendations for re-organising the town's fire brigade.

Plans for an extension to the Guildhall police station at a cost of £4,000, and a second plan for a police fire brigade station in Goat Street at a cost of £3,600, were submitted to the council by the Borough Surveyor at a meeting on 8 March 1882. After a brief discussion, the plans were deferred until a special committee could be convened. After nearly five years in office, it was evident that Captain Colquhoun was not afraid of change. He had gained the respect of all the officers and men, and even some of the councillors.

At about 4am on Wednesday 31 March 1882, Sergeant Eynon, along with constables Williams and Llewellyn, was on the beat in Oxford Street. The men observed smoke issuing from Mr Eva's drapers shop, and it was evident that the fire had been smouldering for some time. They sent a message for the fire brigade, and attempted to warn the occupants. However, before the arrival of the fire brigade, flames broke out from the shop with great violence, and the occupants were in immediate danger. Sergeant Eynon, with great presence of mind, pulled out the canvas blind over the front of the shop, and by this means Mr Eva, his child and some assistants were rescued. A ladder, kept against the nearby market wall for just such an occasion, was brought and placed against the burning building, to rescue the remaining occupants. The fire brigade, under the command of Captain Colquhoun and Inspector Holland, was soon on the scene. With a plentiful supply of water and the chemical fire extinguisher, they confined the blaze to Mr Eva's shop, which unfortunately was totally destroyed.

When Captain Elgee, the Government Inspector, made his annual visit, he included various recommendations in his report to the Watch Committee. They all involved the rectifying of the present police and fire brigade accommodation problems. The borough architect, Mr Cousens, was asked to draw up plans and estimates, in the hope that the council would act on the critical recommendations made. The purchase of the chapel at the rear of the High Street police fire brigade station, and a triangular piece of land abutting Alexandra Road and Pleasant Street, which also included the Ragged School, was considered.

The debate about the provision of more police and fire brigade accommodation continued, and added to this was the belief of some councillors that Swansea was in need of more central municipal offices, as the Guildhall was too far from the centre of the town. The head constable, in his January 1883 report, reiterated his recommendations of July 1880, about the need for a more central police fire brigade station, the position of fire hydrants and street fire escapes, including ladders, and their locations. He favoured the Alexandra Road site for a new central police fire brigade station. Within a quarter of a mile of the Guildhall there were two constable's beats and 318 houses, most of which were only stores or offices, but around Alexandra Road there were six constable's beats and 615 houses, with a greater number of inhabitants.

Following this revelation by the head constable, the committee's attention was directed to other matters, particularly the tragic fire at 62 Lower Oxford Street, where two young men lost their lives.

The fire broke out at around 1am on Sunday 20 January 1883. Constable Jones (36), who was on duty in Hospital Square, St Helen's Road, noticed a light in the window of Williams's Ironmonger and Hardware shop, at the corner of Lower Oxford Street and Beach Street. Along with two civilians, Mr Lawrence and Mr Collins, Constable Jones went to investigate. The shop was on fire, and Collins was sent to raise the fire brigade, while PC Jones and Lawrence broke down the door. With the arrival of the fire brigade came the customary crowds, all shouting and giving instructions. Unfortunately, the fire brigade were confronted with the usual delay in obtaining water. In the meantime, rescues were made. Ladders were placed to the windows and constables ascended. The first to enter the burning upstairs room was PC Williams (46). His hair and eyebrows were burnt, but he returned to the window and handed out a young child, whom he had found lying in the middle of the room. With the crowds still shouting, informing the firemen that there was still a child in the building, Constables Williams and Parry climbed the ladder, closely followed by PC James Dee. The fire was burning quite fiercely, and PC Parry, with one leg in through the window, said that he could see the second child. PC Dee placed his hands on the shoulders of PC Parry, and lifted himself up and into the burning room via the window. After rescuing the child, PC Dee returned to the window to hand him to PC Parry, then re-entered the room to check no one remained inside. Unfortunately, neither child survived the blaze despite the valiant efforts of PC Dee, who was himself confined to hospital with severe burns to his face and hands.

Once a substantial supply of water was obtained, the fire was finally extinguished. The turncock, a Mr Argent, when questioned during the Coroners inquest about the delay of water at the fire, stated that he had only taken 12 minutes to re-direct the water supply, which had required the operating of valves in Wyndham Street, Dillwyn Street, Richardson Street, Beach Street, Bond Street, Fleet Street, St Helen's Crescent, St Helen's Avenue and Gorse Lane. The Water Works Company's need to turn off the supply at night, which led to the delay in obtaining water for the fire brigade, was blamed by some for the children's death. The accusations led the council to announce that they, along with the Water Works Co., would look into the delay and the costs of the fire.

In February the council received a letter from the Royal Society for the Protection of Life from Fire in London, requesting information about the rescues performed by Police Constable James Dee. Captain Colquhoun recommended that the committee inform the Home Secretary of the constable's bravery, with a view to Dee being presented with the Royal Albert Medal.

Captain Colquhoun went on to state that the serious nature of the fire and the number of appliances that were required showed that there was not sufficient manpower. He considered the matter so serious, that he again brought to the attention of the committee his reports of 13 February, 31 May and 6 July 1880.

The mayor, in his report on the fire, remarked that as soon as he had heard the distressing news of the fire, he had visited the scene. He spoke personally to Mr Williams, the shop owner and father of the deceased boys. During the conversation Mr Williams praised the police for their gallant attempts to rescue his boys, but thought that they might have been saved if a supply of water had been obtained earlier. This prompted the mayor to say that 'he had never been more disgusted in his life to hear such a statement, after the enormous amount of money which had been spent in the Borough, they found that there was only sufficient force of water to throw a supply some 12 feet high.'

This statement by the mayor, coupled with the head constable's remarks about insufficient manpower, provoked heated discussion in the council chamber. The meeting concluded that the head constable should be asked to submit a full report on his recommendations for the re-organising of the fire brigade. The committee also recommended that the Town Clerk inform the Home Secretary of Police Constable Dee's heroic conduct at the recent Oxford Street fire.

At a council meeting on Wednesday 14 February, the Town Clerk read out a letter that had been received from Sir W.C. Harcourt, which said that PC 71 James Leach Dee was to be awarded with the Albert Medal, Second Class. The *London Gazette* reported on 20 February 1883:

Whitehall, 19 February, 1883.

The Queen has been graciously pleased to confer the 'Albert Medal, of the Second Class,' upon James Dee, a Constable of the Swansea Police Force, for conspicuous gallantry displayed in endeavouring to save life at a fire, which occurred on the morning of Sunday, 20 January last.

The Albert Medal was named after Prince Albert, the Prince Consort, who died in 1861. When it was instituted in 1866 it was awarded for gallantry in saving life at sea. It was then extended in 1867 to cover actions on land. The general esteem that the award was held in earned it the unofficial name of the civilian VC (Victoria Cross). Like the VC, the decoration entitled one to a gratuity irrespective of class.

The head constable, on 9 March 1883, informed the Watch Committee that he had received a letter from the Royal Society for the Protection of Life from Fire, asking that they be furnished with the names of the constables who assisted PC Dee at the Oxford Street fire (namely Parry, Payne and Williams), so that they could issue a certificate testifying their bravery, and a gratuity of £4. The civilians who had assisted at the fire were recognised by a gratuity from the council. Mr W.E. Burgess, Mr T. Collins and Mr Huggleston were awarded £1 1s (1 guinea) each, Messrs Harris, Franze and Moor were awarded half a guinea (10s 6d) and a further gratuity of £20 was awarded to the Swansea Hospital, for the care and attention they gave to the sufferers.

On Wednesday 21 March 1883, the main entrance to the Guildhall was the scene of a public presentation. The *Cambrian* newspaper reported that between 2,000 and 3,000 people turned out to watch the mayor and mayoress honour Swansea's heroes. The first presentation was of the Albert Medal and its £50 gratuity, and a testimonial and gratuity from the Royal Society for the Protection of Life from Fire and Swansea Town Council to PC 71 James Leach Dee. A testimonial and £4 gratuity was then awarded to Constables Parry, Payne and Williams.

There was then a further presentation to the survivors of the Mumbles lifeboat (the *Wolverhampton*), who earlier that year had responded to the *Prinz Albert,* in difficulties off the Mumbles. The lifeboat's captain, Mr Jenkin Jenkins (who lost two sons, members of the crew, during the disaster), was awarded the medal of the Royal National Lifeboat Institution, and £50. Also mentioned for their bravery in that rescue attempt were the *Wolverhampton*'s crew, Gunner Edward Hutchings of the Mumbles Battery, and two sisters, Mrs Wright and Miss Ace, who although not present at the ceremony had assisted Gunner Hutchings. Captain Jenkin Jenkins, during his command of the lifeboat, had been responsible for saving 63 lives.

It was also reported at the ceremony that, on 6 April 1883, another fireman, Superintendent Kemp of the Worcester Fire Brigade, had been awarded the Albert Medal for bravery at a fire in Halesowen.

The mayor, in his address to the Town Council on 11 April, informed them that he had been presented with a painting of the presentation of awards at the Guildhall on 21 March, and with the Council's consent he would hang the picture on the wall of the council chamber.

With the presentations and award ceremonies over, the Watch Committee resumed debate of the proposals relating to the increase in police and fire brigade accommodation. At the April meeting the committee was informed that they would be approaching Her Majesty's Treasury for the money to fund the building proposals. The financial breakdown for the proposals was: alterations at the Guildhall £2,000, accommodation for council purposes £4,600. The council owned certain houses in Goat Street, which were available for conversion into a central police and fire brigade station. The estimated cost for the converting of these two houses was £750. Thus the total costs amounted to £7,350.

Swansea Council was still attempting to put off the inevitable, but in the meantime the town was once again hit by fire. A serious blaze broke out on

Monday 4 June 1883, when at 2.58pm a message was conveyed to the High Street fire station, informing them of a fire at 'Little Dustpan' a hardware store in High Street. The fire, which was in a wooden tar-coated shed at the rear of the premises, was well alight. Within 10 minutes, a standpipe had been shipped (fixed into the mains) and a jet was playing on the flames. The Guildhall and Oxford Street appliances arrived, but the fire had reached alarming proportions, spreading throughout the building. The whole premises was a mass of flames. The firemen trained several powerful jets on the building, but the effects were not encouraging, and the whole district was shrouded in thick black smoke. It was soon apparent to all that the 'Little Dustpan' was beyond saving. The firemen were forced to concentrate their efforts on confining the blaze, to prevent it spreading to the adjoining premises.

The usual hordes of onlookers were present. The fire brigade was assisted by members of the Ben Evans & Co. Drapery Store, who were said to be using their 'patent chemical extinguishers'. (These would probably have been the two-gallon 'Minimax' soda acid extinguishers.) Other helpers acted as a 'salvage corps', rescuing stock and furniture. The fire was finally subdued by 5pm, although it was not totally extinguished until 11pm, some eight hours later. The estimated cost of the fire and water damage amounted to between £2,500 and £3,000.

Police Constable Dee was the focus of attention again on 8 August, this time for all the wrong reasons. The Watch Committee had to deal with a complaint against PC Dee's conduct. He was accused of visiting public houses while on duty, and on the evening of 6 August of assaulting, without cause, certain persons in Oxford Street. After taking into consideration all the known facts, and the evidence submitted, as well as the constable's previous good character, the Watch Committee decided that instead of dismissing Dee from the force, they would fine him £1 and demote him two grades to second class constable. There

would be a corresponding decrease in his pay. However, on 24 August the *Cambrian* reported that Dee had in fact been dismissed from the force. Apparently, he had been found guilty of attempting to procure untrue testimony in relation to proceedings under the licensing acts. The head constable, Captain Colquhoun, dismissed him from the force on Tuesday 4 September 1883. It was a sorry end to a heroic career.

Certain members of the Watch Committee had suggested that Dee be given the opportunity to resign, but Captain Colquhoun replied that giving him the option to resign could mean that he would be eligible to join another force. Dismissal was a more punitive measure.

The seventh clause of the original Royal Warrant for the issuing of the Albert Medal stated that: 'any recipient guilty of any crime or disgraceful conduct, shall forthwith be erased from the registry of individuals, and his medal shall be forfeited.' However, in D.V. Henderson's *In Heroic Endeavours,* a complete register of the Albert, Edward and Empire gallantry medals and how they were won, there is no record of former PC James Leach Dee ever having his Albert Medal rescinded.

The head constable, in his monthly report to the Watch Committee, mentioned that the Goat Street police fire brigade station was nearing completion. He considered it necessary that it be connected to the other stations. Although the ABC telegraphic system was a good one, it was not as efficient as the new telephone system, so the head constable thought that the new system should be adopted, and alarm bells should be installed in his residence as well as the other stations, including the residence of Superintendent George Holland. The annual cost of this would be £65. The Watch Committee, on the head constable's recommendation, decided to adopt the proposed scheme.

Captain Colquhoun also informed the committee that the force required four extra men, to staff the new

Goat Street police fire brigade station. Money would be available from the Home Office to fund the positions, which would not have been the case had the new officers been employed exclusively as fire brigade personnel. He also pointed out that the new station in Goat Street could not house all the fire brigade's appliances and equipment. This outraged some councillors, who claimed that if they had been aware of this they would not have voted for a new central station. The head constable said that a Mr Lloyd, of Oxford Street, had offered to provide stable accommodation for the prison van and a fire engine, for 5s 6d. He would also supply horses for fire brigade use at a charge of £10 per annum. The committee had no real alternative but to accept the head constable's recommendations.

Wassail Street was the next locality to fall victim to an outbreak of fire. At 7.30am on Friday 31 October 1884, a serious fire occurred at another drapery store, the Drapery Emporium of Perkins and Smith. The fire brigade arrived promptly with a hose and reel, although there is no mention of an engine being present. They experienced the usual delay in obtaining a good water supply, and with little or no water and no pressure, they could only watch as the fire raged unchecked and gained a firm hold on the premises. The adjoining premises of Mr Evans and Mr Hansard were now in imminent danger. It was not until around 8.15am that an adequate supply of water was obtained, which enabled the fire brigade to extinguish the flames.

The loss of the two young boys at the Oxford Street fire was still uppermost in the minds of the Watch Committee when the head constable informed them that if it had not been for an ex-constable, Mr Davies, now in the employ of Mr Hansard, the Wassail Street fire, like the one in Oxford Street, would have resulted in loss of life. Mr Davies had climbed to an upstairs room and directed Mrs Perkins and her child to a place of safety. They climbed out of a skylight and across into the next house. He was assisted by a Mr Glover.

The new Goat Street police fire brigade station was now in the final stages of construction, and was nearly ready for the fire brigade and its appliances and equipment to move in. The building was described as:

> ...arranged for the occupancy of nine men, eight unmarried and one married man, these were to form the fire brigade proper, and on the members of the Police Force will be 'Told off' in the event of a fire, where they will prevent interference or crashing. This along with the possibility in the near future of an abundant supply of water, the Fire Brigade would be equipped to deal with any emergency.

The first fire that the new Goat Street fire brigade station was called to attend occurred at 4.20am on 24 December 1884. PC 82 Edwards observed smoke issuing from Mr Goldstone's tobacconists in St Mary's Street. After alerting the occupants, PC Edwards, who had been joined by PC 32 Jones, sent for the ladder, which was stored in the nearby castle yard. Unfortunately, an 18-year-old assistant named Phillip Freeman, who lived over the tobacconists, jumped from the second floor window in panic. He landed heavily on the pavement below and fractured his skull. He was carried into a neighbours house, where he died of his injuries. The ladder arrived too late for the young assistant, but not for Mr Goldstone, his wife and a female assistant, who were rescued. The fire, which had originated in a downstairs room, was extinguished by the firemen.

A mock fire to test the brigade's efficiency took place on 5 February 1885. The imaginary fire was at the premises of Sir. H.H. Vivian at Parkwern, near Sketty, which at that time was just outside the borough boundary. The alarm was given at the Goat Street station at 2.31pm, whereby the members of the fire brigade were dispatched to the Oxford Street section house, arriving there at 2.36pm. In the meantime, the engine had been horsed and was ready

Singleton Abbey, the scene of a serious fire in February 1896. (Author's collection)

to go. The brigade set off at a gallop to Parkwern, where they arrived at 2.45pm, some nine minutes after they were dispatched from the Oxford Street station, and 14 minutes after the initial alarm was received at Goat Street. Three lengths of hose were connected to an ample supply of water, which was then pumped over the simulated fire. By this time it was eight minutes to three, 23 minutes since the departure from Swansea. The head constable and Superintendent Holland supervised the exercise, which involved 12 members of the borough fire brigade.

After the exercise the fire brigade proceeded to another of the Vivian properties, where means of escape from fire were tested. This involved several of the staff employed at the abbey jumping from the upper storeys into a 'jump sheet', used by the fire

brigade for rescues. On the conclusion of the exercises it was reported that the tests had been efficient, prompt and satisfactory.

Morriston, although surrounded by heavy industry, had limited resources for fighting fires, and on 14 March 1885 a large fire was occurred in a drapers in Woodfield Street, which in a short space of time engulfed the whole property. The alarm was raised at the Morriston police fire brigade station in Martin Street, and prompted the arrival of Inspector Williams and two constables, who trained jets of water on the front and rear of the property. The water pressure was not good, and Inspector Williams directed his efforts to saving some young people whose lives were in imminent danger. Within 45 minutes the Swansea fire brigade, under the command of Captain Colquhoun, arrived on the scene. They set to work, making an immediate impact. The mayor arrived and brought with him in his carriage the patent extinguisher from the Forest Works in Morriston. All that was left of the drapers shop after the fire was the front wall, which had to be demolished for safety reasons. The bill for the fire damage was some £4,000.

On 9 November 1885, a detachment of men from the Swansea fire brigade, under the command of Inspector Flynn, visited London to take part in the Lord Mayor's Parade. As a result they received a testimonial admitting them as a member of the Fire Brigades Association.

On 15 January 1886, the *Cambrian* reported on the efficiency of the town's brigade under Captain Colquhoun's leadership. In a testimonial it stated that:

> The Swansea Fire Brigade is an institution that deserves the approbation of the whole town. Since it commenced under its present form it has done its work with zeal and efficiency, that leaves little more to be desired. Especially during the last six months have its capabilities been shown, and shown in such a way as to draw forth expressions of praise from the authorities, from the press, and from the public in general. During that time there has unfortunately been no dearth of fires in the town, yet in no instance, whether by day or by night, has the Brigade been found wanting, in speed, strength or competency. If a fire occurs even in the middle of the night, the men at the station where the alarm is first given are up, dressed, and on the scene with the necessary appliances, almost before the alarm has been communicated to the other stations, and by the time that reinforcements have arrived the extinguishing operations are

in full swing. This was capitally demonstrated the other night in the case of a fire which broke out on premises in Oxford Street. The Alarm was received at the Guildhall Police Station at ten minutes to 11 o'clock from the Section House, (Oxford Street) whence the reels had already been despatched to the scene of the fire. In something under five minutes this contingent was joined by the reels from Goat Street Station, and a little later on by the apparatus from the Guildhall. Little wonder then, that the flames, already fierce were completely extinguished in less than five and twenty minutes from the time the reaching the Guildhall. This extraordinary fleetness is due to the careful training which each member of the brigade had received under the Head Constable (Captain Colquhoun), Superintendent George Holland and Inspector Flynn, all of whom evidently take pride in the Superiority of their men. During the time mentioned we have had fires in the day and night, on board ships, in dwelling houses, in works, and in shops containing inflammable and non-inflammable materials, yet the whole of the damage done would probably not exceed that of one good Metropolitan conflagration, a blessing for which we owe the Swansea Fire Brigade a debt of gratitude. All this is the meritorious in them, when it is considered that they lack the apparatus which even a town like Cardiff possesses, and we believe, an equal number of men.

On 22 January 1886, a report appeared in the *Cambrian* announcing the death of ex-Inspector Ball, who was one of those who commended for his bravery in effecting rescues at the tragic fire in Temple Street, on 10 May 1866. Ball had retired prematurely from the force, after he was injured when a wall collapsed on him at a fire in Hanover Street.

Some of Swansea's outlying districts had little or no fire cover, and when a fire did occur, fighting it was left to the occupants, neighbours and the local beat constable, who, other than ensuring that the premises had been vacated, or rescuing the people within, could do little. One such fire, on Thursday 19 May 1887 in the village of Mumbles, was for some reason not attended by the Swansea fire brigade, although they had responded to other 'outside' fires, at even greater distances. Mumbles was approximately five miles west of Swansea. The building which caught fire was Norton Lodge, a mansion owned by Mr Thomas Millward. The fire was discovered at about 1.30am by Mrs Millward, who had been awakened by the sound of crackling, and had found the house well alight. After alerting the rest of the household, she made good her escape. Nearly an hour elapsed before PC Hopkins, of the county constabulary, arrived with his sergeant and a detachment of the Mumbles coastguard, superintended by Captain Godfrey. With no means for extinguishing the fire at hand, their only option was to resort to forming a bucket chain from the nearby Swansea Bay. The fire by this time was at its height, illuminating the whole of the neighbourhood. All that was able to burn was totally consumed, and within a few hours only a smouldering ruin was left.

Even when fire appliances and equipment were available, difficulties were still sometimes experienced, as the Swansea fire brigade found to its cost over the years. On the night of Wednesday 28 June 1887, reports were received at the Guildhall station that a serious fire had started near the Midland Railway Station in the St Thomas district. After informing the other stations, Inspector Flynn responded. On arrival he was confronted by volumes of thick black smoke, and on closer inspection he perceived that the fire had broken out on the premises of Mr Paton's ironmongers shop, which was situated in the New Cut Road, near the railway station. Standpipes were shipped at the corner, adjacent to the station, and in Foxhole Road, and hoses attached, but there was no water available. Even the tank at the railway station was dry, and the manual engine, with several lengths of suction attached, was set into the nearby River Tawe. Unfortunately, as the river is tidal, and the tide was out, a sufficient force of water could not be obtained. The small quantity of water that was available was played on the coffee shop and adjoining premises. The premises of Mr Eastman, greengrocer, and Mr Andrews, fishmonger, were by now well alight, and the decision was taken to reposition the engine slightly further down river near the Cuba Hotel, although this had little effect. Captain Colquhoun then ordered the engine to be moved near to the Duke's Arch, where he seconded a relief of men from the Great Western Railway to operate the pumping handles. The move did have the desired effect, and with the efforts of the men a good pressure and supply was eventually secured.

The fire was still raging, and had consumed most of the buildings. Roofs and floors had fallen in, and the firemen did not succeed in extinguishing the flames until 11.30pm. By then all that was left was a smouldering mass.

The head constable, in his monthly report to the Watch Committee in August, informed the meeting of the difficulties experienced at the recent fire in St Thomas. The report was discussed and some councillors proposed the linking of the Water Works Co. and the fire brigade station by telephone to alleviate the problems. Captain Colquhoun disagreed, and recommended that Swansea purchase a steam fire engine. In the meantime, the manual engine would still be used at fires. The cost of manpower for the operation of the handles at the recent St Thomas fire had been £7 10s 6d, paid to the workers of the Great Western Railway Company. Captain Colquhoun believed that it was necessary to install fire hydrants, which should be inserted into the mains at intervals of every 200 or 300 yards.

Captain Colquhoun stressed that the town was in dire need of better fire precautions and appliances. If his recommendation to install fire hydrants was taken up by the committee, it would overcome the problems encountered by the brigade at fires, and result in a copious supply of water. This would allow the engines to be operated more effectively, removing the need for an expensive steam-powered fire engine, which would also incur the added expense of employing two engineers.

In conclusion to his report Captain Colquhoun informed the meeting that at present the fire brigade consisted of 20 men, although this number was often reduced at times of fire, as they were scattered about the town. The manual engine required up to 22 men to operate it, so force numbers ought to be increased by 12 to ensure adequate manpower. Constables should also be provided with cheque books so that they could employ extra men at fires if required. In addition, a more efficient system was needed to supply horses for fire brigade work, instead of the present agreement with Mr Lloyd of Oxford Street. Captain Colquhoun believed that the corporation would be able to obtain a government grant of £32 per annum, which would enable the police and fire brigade to keep three horses for mounted patrols, the fire engine, and the prison van and ambulance (also the responsibility of the police).

In nearly ten years as head constable, Captain Colquhoun had achieved a great deal in relation to the town's provision for fire cover and precautions. He continued to make recommendations for the re-organisation of the fire brigade, highlighting the need for the provision of an engine shed, stables and yard. A convenient site was available opposite the present Goat Street police fire brigade station, at a cost of

£160. Alternatively, they could rent part of the lower section at the rear of the Agricultural Hall, in St Helen's Road (old Eddershaw's store), for the same purpose. This site was at the rear of the Oxford Street section house. He also proposed the purchase of another manual engine at a cost not exceeding £120.

The committee debated the head constable's recommendations, and decided that the borough surveyor should prepare estimates for the installation of fire hydrants. The committee granted £120 for another manual engine, although some councillors thought that the St Thomas district would benefit most from this addition. It also agreed to the employment of 12 additional constables at a cost of 1s each.

Alderman Daniel remarked that it would have been better and more cost-effective for the corporation to purchase another patent fire extinguisher. Another councillor, Mr Tutton, said that he was dissatisfied with the head constable's report, and would like a further report to be submitted, detailing how many fires, day and night, the brigade attended. This could then be discussed at a further meeting. In response to these criticisms the head constable replied: '... that the whole difficulty in regard to the extinction of fires, was the scarcity of water, in relation to the patent fire extinguisher, extinguishers were good in rooms or at the commencement of fires, but were practically useless at large fires.'

The proposal for providing accommodation for the engine and stables was rejected, and the committee accepted Mr Lloyd's offer to provide horses for the fire brigade, day and night, at a cost of £1 11s 6d per week, and accommodation for fire appliances and the prison van at 9s 6d per week. The provision of fire hydrants arose again at the Watch Committee meeting of 22 August, when the decision was taken to extend the water main from Portland Street to Goat Street, and to install 10 fire hydrants along its length. A branch water main would be laid from the south entrance of the cricket field, to the Cricketers Arms in King Edward's Road, and two hydrants installed, with further hydrants and valves installed in the Cwmdonkin main at the foot of Bryn-y-mor Lane, and another at the junction at Walter Road. It was also decided that fire hydrants would be installed along the whole length of the high level main from Morriston, through Bryhyfryd to Carmarthen Road, at distances not exceeding 200 yards apart. Where convenient they would be placed at the corners of streets. This breakthrough was one of the biggest achievements of Captain Colquhoun's 36-year career.

In October the head constable was authorised to rent an archway in Fabian Street, in the St Thomas district, for the housing of a fire engine. This coincided with the town's purchase of a new manual fire engine. A report on a fire that occurred on 14 December 1887 at the Dyffryn Tin Plate Works in Morriston stated: 'The new fire engine was sent from Swansea'. The engine travelled from Swansea to the scene of the fire, some four miles, in a remarkable 14 minutes.

The head constable's monthly report to the Watch Committee on 23 March 1888 included the need for Swansea to acquire a steam fire engine. He revealed that Messrs Merryweather's, the famous London fire engine manufacturers, could supply a steam fire engine at a cost of £450, with an allowance of £129 against the recently purchased manual. If purchased, he suggested that the rear part of the Agricultural Hall, as previously recommended, be rented and adapted for its storage. The mayor recommended that the proposal be adopted by the committee, and most councillors agreed. The Town Clerk reported at the next meeting that the local government had sanctioned a loan of £450 for the purchase of a steam fire engine, repayable over 10 years. Councillor Chapman objected, saying that there was little value in spending £450 on a steam fire engine, unless assurances could be given that a continuous water supply in the town's mains was available. Mr Wyrill,

the borough engineer, replied that a continuous supply was not currently available, and was unlikely to be in the near future, until a new reservoir at Morriston was completed. The chairman of the committee then proposed that the borrowing of the £450 from the local government be abandoned, and the motion was carried by nine votes to seven.

Mr Lloyd's contract with the council to supply horses for the fire brigade was terminated on 19 October 1888 under a three-month notice agreement, when it was decided that the head constable be given £120 per annum for the purchase of two horses for fire brigade and mounted patrol duties.

The local newspaper reported in January 1889 that:

> The new Fire Brigade engine, with its two new horses and harnesses were inspected by members of the Corporation in the Guildhall Yard, the horses were in the charge of, and driven by Police Constable Johns and showed splendid action, the harnesses and accoutrements were supplied by Mr Pike, Union Street, were scrupulously clean and reflected credit upon Constable Williams (46) the engineer, who was in charge of that department. Both officers were in uniform and Inspector Davies who is in charge of the Fire Brigade was also in attendance. The Members (Councillors) after making a careful inspection, expressed their opinion that the engine and horses were worthy of the Corporation and the Town.

Although the above report mentions 'the engineer', at this time the fire engines were manual, and a steam engine did not arrive until 1906.

It was not only the newspapers that took an avid interest in fire brigade affairs. In February 1889 a local theatre was showing a farce, *The Still Alarm*, about life in the fire brigade. This interest in the fire brigade reflected well on Captain Colquhoun's direction of the town's firefighting services.

In May 1889, Captain Colquhoun travelled to London in his capacity as chief of the Swansea Fire Brigade. He noted and took a special interest in the organisation and workings of the London Fire Brigade, whose chief at the time was the famous Eyre Massey Shaw, hoping to benefit the Swansea brigade. During his stay in the capital he also took part in Queen Victoria's 70th birthday celebrations.

Captain Colquhoun obviously won his argument with the Watch Committee about alterations at the rear Agricultural Hall in order to house the manual engine. In July 1889, a fire occurred at the same location as the previous fire involving three shops and the Midland Railway Station. The report into the fire stated that the manual engine and reels had turned out from the Oxford Street section house. The fire was of a less serious character than the one that had occurred in June 1887, and a plentiful supply of water was available. The fire was soon extinguished.

The advantages of an unlimited supply of manpower to operate the pumping handles were demonstrated at a fire at the Pascoe Grenfell Copper Works in Upper Bank, near Pentrechwyth, on 5 July 1889. The fire brigade were telephoned for by the works system, and attended promptly. A report stated 'On receipt of the alarm at the Fire Brigade Depot, the engine and hose were at once horsed, and dashing along the road at a terrific rate, were soon at the seat of the fire.' The efficiency of the brigade and the works employees meant that the damage was dramatically reduced, and the fire quickly extinguished. The report concluded that the police, with the exception of those that manned the hose, had a reasonably easy time, as they had no occasion to touch the engine once it had been initially positioned. Hundreds of ready and willing hands were anxious to relieve those on the handles when they showed signs of exhaustion. After about an

hour, the efforts of all those in attendance had extinguished the fire.

With Swansea's population continually on the increase, Captain Colquhoun again stressed the need for extra constables. In September a proposal was carried to increase the force by 12 men, two of whom would be set apart for weights and measures duty. The head constable also mentioned the situation regarding extra men at the Goat Street station. Due to the scarcity of water, the remaining constables would do duty at the Oxford Street section house, as the engine would be attending all fires. The head constable also stated that the Swansea Fire Brigade was as efficient and economical as any other town where the same system existed.

In December, the superintendent of the fire brigade, George Holland, announced his retirement. His pension was set at £1 per week, and he augmented this by continuing as Inspector of Weights and Measures, at a salary of £100 per year. His premature retirement, the committee were informed, was due to his increased infirmity from rheumatic pain, incurred by his frequent wetting, in day or night, by weather and hose, while acting as superintendent of the Swansea Fire Brigade. The committee were informed by the head constable that the estimated cost of maintaining the fire brigade was £463 16s 3d.

The Goat Street fire brigade station, although only built in 1884, had outgrown its usefulness. It had suffered from accommodation and ventilation problems since its opening, although these were the very problems it was supposed to have alleviated. The engine, prison van and stables were originally at the premises of Mr Lloyd in Oxford Street, but after the termination of this contract, the Oxford Street section house accommodated the engine and horses and any extra constables. This was deemed to be an unsatisfactory arrangement, and prompted calls for a purpose-built central police and fire brigade station.

One councillor who supported this proposal was

Mr Gwilym Morgan, and at the Watch Committee meeting on 8 July 1890, he submitted a scheme for a new central police fire brigade station, claiming that it save the corporation considerable expense. It would involve the removal of the smaller stations, concentrating the main body of the force at one location. It would mean that a sufficient number of men could be gathered together quickly in the event of a fire, and that all the fire brigade appliances, equipment and hose could be stored there. The proposal was similar to a recommendation made by Captain Colquhoun on 15 July 1880.

In the early hours of Saturday 29 November 1890 an alarming fire broke out at Parlby's, a chemist's in Mansel Street. The fire brigade attended promptly, and were confronted with flames and smoke issuing from the upper floors. There was great anxiety about a young child and servant who were in the building. Sergeant Parry, who had received many accolades for his bravery, ran to nearby Carlton Terrace for a fire brigade ladder. Three civilians helped him position it against the window of an upper floor. He ascended, entered the smoke-filled room via the window, and after groping about for what seemed an eternity, located the child, Lily Leonard. He then returned to the window and handed the child to a civilian. Sergeant Parry re-entered the room and found the servant, Nellie O'Keefe, who by this time was unconscious. The gallant officer carried her out of the building, down the ladder, to safety.

Captain Colquhoun eulogised the bravery of acting Sergeant Parry at the next Watch Committee meeting in December, and also praised the efforts of the three civilians who had assisted him, Messrs Johns, Mayheu and Prosser Evans, recommending that they be thanked by the council for their efforts. Councillors Howell and Leeder acknowledged that Sergeant Parry had distinguished himself at two previous fires, and as such should be rewarded by being permanently promoted to the rank of sergeant. This popular proposition was instantly agreed to.

The mayor, Mr J.T.D. Llewellyn, at the police court on 31 December 1890, conferred upon Sergeant Parry the bronze medal of the 'Quiver Hero's Fund', for his bravery at the recent Parlby chemist's shop. The Quiver and Answers Heroes' Funds were set up by newspapers to award medals and gratuities to people who had performed acts of bravery. The medal was worn on the right side of the breast, as it was not recognised as an official medal of the realm. Acts of bravery by members of the fire brigade, were well publicised. Police Constable Northcote was praised for his promptness and courage in extinguishing the clothes of a man named Smith, which had caught fire when a paraffin lamp exploded at his shop in the High Street on 28 November 1891. PC 70 Delve and PC 64 Evans were honoured for their part in fighting a fire in Castle Street. On occasion gratitude for bravery was accompanied by a cheque. After the Castle Street fire a cheque for £5 was distributed among the members of the fire brigade that attended. In January, Constable Northcote was also presented with the bronze medal of the 'Quiver Hero's Fund' by the mayor, now a Mr Mason, on behalf of the editor of the said fund.

Heroics and bravery were becoming the hallmark of the Swansea Fire Brigade. On 20 March 1892 there was a serious fire at the Royal Hotel in the High Street. PC 32 Morgan heard the shouts of 'Fire!' while on his beat nearby, and went straight to the scene, where he was informed that the housekeeper, Ann Davies, was still in the burning building. Constable Morgan entered the building and, battling with the suffocating smoke, reached the landing and the housekeeper's room, where he found the woman, clad only in her night attire, in a state of semi-consciousness. He carried her downstairs and out of the building to a place of safety. The head constable, in his next monthly report, recommended to the committee that PC 32 Morgan be awarded a Merit Badge for his meritorious conduct, and this was agreed to. Constable Morgan was also Swansea's first recipient of the bronze medal of 'Answers', a medal like the 'Quiver' previously described.

The Bath & West Agricultural Show visited Swansea's Victoria Park on 3 June 1892, and fire protection was the sole responsibility of Merryweather's and Sons, of Greenwich, London. They installed a temporary fire station in the park, manned by their own firemen, under the command of Captain J.H. Cleaver, late of the Croydon Fire Brigade. The station provoked a great deal of interest, and the chief exhibit on show was the *Greenwich* steam fire engine, capable of pumping 360 gallons per minute. This engine had been supplied to: Bath, Salisbury, Stratford, Hungerford, Coventry, London, Manchester and, most notably, Swansea's neighbour, Briton Ferry. At that time Briton Ferry had its own fire brigade, independent of the police. Merryweather's display also included demonstrations involving their new manual fire engine, as well as their various hoses, standpipes and hose reels.

At the conclusion of the Bath & West Show, Merryweather's attended the Guildhall Yard in Somerset Place, where on 10 June they displayed and exercised their *Greenwich* steam fire engine, with the hope that the Swansea Town Council would purchase one. The test for the steamer took the form of first one jet, then two jets, working up to five jets, which sent forth streams of water that projected well over the Guildhall. The engine got up steam in seven minutes, producing 100psi, with a maximum of five jets at 120psi.

Even after this fine display, some councillors were still sceptical of the merits of the steam engine over the manual engine. These doubts were soon dispelled at a second test that took place at the Ben Evans store in Castle Street. This time the test was to show the superiority of a steam engine over a manual in terms of the manpower required to operate it. At the conclusion of the test the Watch Committee were informed that the cost of a steam fire engine would be £500, although Merryweather's would give an allowance against the present manual engine.

The committee debated the question of the purchase of a steam fire engine at their next meeting on 14 June, and instructed the Town Clerk to make the relevant enquiries of the local government with regard to its purchase. They would offer Merryweather's £400 and the town's present manual engine. The debate, however, continued, as some councillors voiced their doubts. Alderman Locke said that Swansea already had the smartest and most efficient brigade of any its size. Councillor Leeder remarked that the purchase of a steam engine was a luxury that would require men to maintain it, and pointed out that fire insurance companies kept brigades in other towns. Alderman Freeman enquired about where the steamer would be kept, and wondered whether there would be a need to erect a new station. Alderman Pike said that 'before he could pass a judgement, he would like to know, the additional cost of maintaining a steamer? i.e. engineer etc.' The final argument against the purchase of a steam engine came from Councillor Tutton, who said that although he would not like to see lives lost at fires, people did not stay in the burning building, they left by means of the fire escape. With all doubts and objections voiced, the outcome was to refer the decision to another committee, involving members who understood engines.

The debate about purchasing a steam engine continued, and the head constable reported that the annual cost of maintaining a steamer was £150. He further remarked that he would not be held responsible if a serious fire occurred at which a steam engine would have been of use. The chairman agreed with him, but the meeting unfortunately ended with the proposal being deferred.

In April, Captain Colquhoun submitted a report about police numbers, stating that the total strength of the borough force was 99, with nine sergeants, five inspectors, one superintendent, one head constable and 83 constables. Of this number two men were specially employed: four detectives, three clerks, one warrant officer, one at the theatre, eight in charge of streets, seven on reserve, and on average eight off sick or on leave. One officer serves as the head constable's aid. This compared with other towns or cities as follows:

Town	Population	Acres	Police officers
Swansea	90,423	5,963	99
Plymouth	34,179	1,393	103
Bath	51,851	3,745	86
Newport	55,695	4,924	68
Cardiff	128,849	7,374	178

(The number for Cardiff was exclusive of 40 docks police.)

A fire thought to be one of the most difficult ever experienced by the Swansea Brigade occurred on 29 May 1893, in the railway arches near the Weaver's flour mill. The fire was in the No.2 arch, occupied by a Mr David Jones, a boatbuilder. The town's engine, hose and reels were soon in attendance, with jets playing on the flames, but unfortunately, as the woodwork of a nearby building was covered in tar, the fire spread rapidly. Before long, arches 3, 4, 5 and 6 were involved. The firemen were thought to be in danger, as they were working beneath a wooden structure supported on stone pillars, which was in imminent danger of collapsing. Thankfully, the steam fire engine belonging to Weaver's mill was brought in, and its powerful jets, manned by Constable Willis and others, made an immediate impact on the blaze. In the course of two hours, the fire was finally extinguished.

The local *Cambrian* newspaper, in its report on the fire, alluded to Captain Colquhoun's leadership and organisation when it stated that 'Swansea as a town, can now feel, if never before, that under Captain Colquhoun, we have one of the smartest Fire brigades.'

Although the newspapers were singing the head constable's praises, some councillors at the monthly meeting of the Watch Committee were expressing doubts and provoking controversy about a new post that had been created, that of sergeant in charge of the fire brigade. The head constable had recommended that Constable Edwards be promoted to the said rank. In promoting Constable Edwards, certain councillors believed that Captain Colquhoun was overlooking seniority. To this the head constable replied that it was nothing to do with overlooking other constables, but was about promoting the right man for the post. The head constable's decision infuriated certain members, and led to heated exchanges. Allegations were made against some councillors, about them 'hob nobbing' with certain constables on their beats, who knew that their objections would be represented at the council meeting.

The head constable stressed that the promotion of Constable Edwards was not about favouritism or overlooking seniority, it was about finding the right man for the post. PC Edwards had asked permission of the head constable to apply for the post of inspector of the fire brigade in South Shields, and the head constable had asked PC Edwards what he could do to induce him to stay in Swansea. PC Edwards replied that he did not see any future for promotion, but he would rather stay in Swansea as a sergeant than to go to South Shields. If PC Edwards was to leave Swansea, the Head Constable remarked, he would have no other alternative other than to advertise the new post, as PC Edwards was the best-qualified person for the job within the Swansea force. Apart from his police qualities, Edwards was trained in fire brigade duties, and had proved his worth as acting sergeant in charge of the Goat Street fire brigade station. Prior to coming to Swansea, PC Edwards had served with the London Fire Brigade under the famous Captain Shaw.

The disagreement continued until the mayor, in his capacity as chairman, asked for a vote to be taken, which resulted in Constable Edwards promotion to sergeant of the fire brigade. This led to Sergeant Edwards being a prominent force in the Swansea fire brigade for many years.

Superintendent David Jones was in charge of the fire brigade while Captain Colquhoun was in London, when at about 6.20pm on Saturday 17 June 1893, a major fire occurred at the saw mills of Messrs Stone & Forster, tin plate manufacturers, whose yard was situated on the south side of the South Dock. The High Street and Goat Street stations had been alerted by telephone, and the engine, hose and reel were taken to the scene.

The fire was raging fiercely by the time the brigade arrived. It was situated inside a corrugated iron shed, which housed an assortment of steam engines and saws, along with a vast quantity of timber. Although a large contingent of the fire brigade was present, difficulties were experienced with water supply. Only one of the fire plugs on the dock was compatible with the brigade's standpipes. However, the manual engine was set in to the abundant supply of water in the nearby dock basin, and two lengths of suction were attached. Twenty or 30 willing men assisted with the pumping levers, and water jets were immediately forthcoming. PC Tucker and other members of the brigade strenuously endeavoured to subdue the flames with their jets, but they were driven back time and again by the heat, flames and thick choking smoke. Eventually their efforts were rewarded, and some five hours after the discovery of the fire, it was extinguished. However, it was deemed advisable to maintain a standpipe and hose in readiness, in case any further outbreaks occurred in the smouldering ruins. This situation continued until 6am on Sunday, nearly 12 hours later. The destruction caused by the fire led to many job losses.

Two months later, on 25 August, Swansea encountered another severe fire. Just after 7pm on Friday evening, a blaze broke out on the premises of Messrs Spiller & Baker, in Little Wind Street. It was reported that '... the fire had the rapidity of extension, and destruction, has not had its parallel in the history of the Town for the last century.' Little Wind Street was a narrow street some few paces wide, which was fronted on one side by the Great Western Railway, which ran on an elevated line supported by brick arches. There were a few cottages, and at one end the Colosseum Hotel and a huge warehouse, which was the scene of the fire.

By the time the brigade arrived on the scene, the fire had taken a firm hold. Flames reached some 50ft into the air. The whole of the fire brigade was in attendance, along with the two engines, hose carts and other equipment. Their task from the outset was daunting, and within a short space of time the roof had collapsed, showering burning debris into the streets, narrowly missing Sergeant Edwards and some of the other constables who had been directing their jets into the burning building from the street below. A decision was soon made for the firemen to concentrate their efforts on confining the blaze in order to save the adjoining premises. Thankfully on this occasion there was a plentiful supply of water from the mains, and standpipes were set into hydrants in many different streets. The police report stated that no fewer than 70 hydrants were used. The borough police were assisted by the docks police, and the fire was eventually subdued by 10pm, but not before the building, which had covered some half an acre, was reduced to a blackened shell of smouldering ruins, enclosed by four grim, gaunt walls.

The fire could be seen from all over the town, and even travellers entering Swansea from Ilfracombe commented on the glare which had illuminated the whole district. A local newspaper reported that, with the usual hoards of townsfolk congregating from all over at the scene, some several thousand people had witnessed the blaze. The fire brigade's hose could still be seen in the street nearly a week later, in case of any further flames from within the smouldering debris.

Another bravery award was conferred on a member of the Swansea fire brigade when on 20 September 1893, Constable Tucker was awarded the bronze medal of the 'Quiver Hero's Fund', for his courage in rescuing a three-year-old child from a smoke-filled house in Tontine Street, Swansea. Constable Tucker had entered the house and, after searching the bedroom, located the child, Richard John Davies, and carried him out. The presentation, which was conducted by the mayor, was also informed that PC Tucker had been instrumental in the saving seven other persons from possible death, four from fire and three from drowning.

The brigade, who had been having quite a busy time of it, were rewarded on 3 February 1894 with a pay-rise. The decision was made by the Watch Committee, after a recommendation from Captain Colquhoun, to increase the firemen's allowance from 1s to 1s 6d, putting them on the same scale as Cardiff.

The Swansea brigade had to travel outside the borough boundary to attend their next blaze. On 31 August 1894, they were called to a fire at Gorseinon, a village approximately seven miles from Swansea. A telephone message had been received at the London & North Western Railway police office at the Victoria Railway Station in Swansea, saying that a serious fire had broken out at the premises of Mr Timothy Jones, grocer, and Mr Vincent Jones, draper, in the High Street, Gorseinon. The Swansea fire brigade were then alerted. The engine was horsed and, under the command of Sergeant Edwards, they departed for the fire. Due to the distance, four horses were required. The crew, which consisted of Sergeant Edwards and Constables Johns and Harris, arrived within about half an hour of receiving the call. On the way they were delayed by the roadway, which was virtually impassable because the contents of the shops had been deposited there. Some men present demanded beer

before they would assist in the manning of the engine's pumping levers. When they eventually got to work, with an ample supply of water from the nearby River Lliw, jets were soon playing on the burning shops. Both roofs were smashed in to facilitate the jets reaching their target, but it soon became apparent that all hope of saving the shops had gone, leaving the firemen no other option than to concentrate on saving the adjoining properties. With the fire extinguished, the brigade returned to Swansea at 7.30am, some seven hours after receiving the call. The estimated cost of damage to the properties was £2,000.

Captain Colquhoun reported in January 1895 that the sum of £205 3s 7d had been expended on the erection of an engine house and other alterations to the Oxford Street section house. He thought that this sum was not excessive, as the section house was served by 13 resident fire brigade men and a turn-cock, and housed the town's manual fire engines.

At future committee meetings the head constable continued to make recommendations relating to the upkeep of the stations and fire brigade equipment. In April 1895, he brought to the council's attention the need for ongoing repairs to the stations, following the government inspection, and alluded to the need for a new fire escape. The escape at the High Street station was now over 30 years old, and ought to be condemned and replaced with a new, 30ft, wheeled escape, which could easily be taken to the scene of a fire. This was agreed to, and an order was placed with Messrs Rose of Manchester. In June a tender was accepted from Messrs Rose for the purchase of a 36ft Kingston fire escape ladder at a cost of £40.

Ben Evans, Swansea's largest drapery store, was very fire conscious, and constantly purchasing and exhibiting extinguishers and rescue apparatus. In August their new fire chute was on display, which would allow people to be rescued from the upper floors, by sliding down the inside of the chute to the ground floor. An article appeared in the *South Wales*

Daily Post, which although it praised the Ben Evans store for their fire precautions, condemned the Swansea Corporation, which, as the Town Council, ought to be responsible for supplying the necessary equipment for rescues from fire, which should be operated by the town's fire brigade. It went on to state that a fire escape capable of reaching Swansea's tallest buildings should be purchased. One of these was the Ben Evans store, which was 70ft high. This was a matter of urgency, as the store had 150 assistants, most of whom resided on the premises.

Swansea, as a seaport, encountered many fires on board ships. In the early hours of Saturday morning on 6 July 1895, the Swansea fire brigade was called to the scene of an explosion aboard the SS *Barbadian*, which was lying in the East Dock. The explosion occurred in the stoke hole after a build up of bunker gas, and the fire, although considered serious, was extinguished in a relatively short space of time. However, four of the ship's crew suffered extensive burns, and tragically, due to the extent of their injuries, two crew members, George Jones, aged 22 and Joseph Dibell, aged 35, both of Kirkdale in Liverpool, died in the Swansea Hospital.

The *Barbadian* was the first of a series of serious ship fires that occurred in 1895. Some, again like the *Barbadian*, were also attended by tragic circumstances. On the morning of 11 July, the barque *Helmi* from Finland, which was lying in the North Dock, was involved in a fire following an explosion which, it was thought resulted from the decanting of petroleum from a cask into tins. The ship's boatswain, a seaman by the name of Klingberg, was severely burnt, and some of his ship mates, Pajarinen and Pakkanen, received superficial burns.

The third explosion occurred on board the steamer *Isobel* on 22 December, while she was lying in the Prince of Wales Dock, and resulted in a coal trimmer, William Steel, of Spring Terrace in Swansea, being burnt on the face and arms. He was taken to Swansea Hospital.

Although these ship fires had required the attendance of the Swansea fire brigade, they had been extinguished in a comparatively short space of time, unlike the second fire that occurred in December. The fire occurred on board the SS *Chatsworth* from Cardiff, which had been lying in the North Dock, and was confined to her port bunker, which was laden with coal. The fire brigade, under the command of Captain Colquhoun, had encountered great difficulty in reaching the steamer, as she was lying away from the wharf. The fullness of the hold meant that the fire could not be reached through the hatches, so in typical fire brigade fashion, the deck was torn up, enabling the firemen to grapple with the fire. By sheer hard work, the firemen's efforts were rewarded, and they were able to subdue and eventually extinguish the outbreak, thus preventing severe and extensive damage to the ship. Thankfully, on this occasion, the fire was not accompanied by death or injury.

After these fires, the head constable informed the Watch Committee that the hydrants on the dock-side had not been compatible with the brigade's equipment, and recommended that the Harbour Trust be contacted with the view to the hydrants being altered. This recommendation was agreed to, but because of the number of ship fires that had occurred in the port, certain councillors were of the opinion that the owners of the ships concerned should be contacted, with the view to a charge or levy being imposed to offset the expenses incurred by the fire brigade in extinguishing the ship fires. Some councillors even likened the extinguishing of fires on board ships to that of claiming salvage at sea. As a result of the council's debate, the Town Clerk was instructed to contact other towns in order to ascertain what action was taken by them when they were confronted with the same circumstances.

Sergeant Payne, who as a police constable had been involved in fighting many of Swansea's fires, including the Oxford Street fire in January 1883, for which he was commended, retired in January 1896. His retirement resulted in a discussion at the Watch Committee meeting, about whether or not his superannuation (pension) should include his fire brigade pay, which at the time was 1s 6d per week. The head constable informed the meeting that Sergeant Payne had completed upwards of 26 years service, and as a result, should be paid two-thirds pension, amounting to 25s 8d per week, and as a member of the fire brigade should also be paid the same two-thirds of that pay, 1s per week extra. Councillor Leeder however, suggested that the Town Clerk contact the Home Office to find out their stance on the matter. This was agreed to, and Sergeant Payne was paid his normal police pension, excluding his fire brigade contributions.

Singleton Abbey, a large mansion and the ancestral home of the late Lord Swansea, Mr H.H. Vivian, fell prey to an extensive and serious fire on Tuesday 4 February 1896. Between 4 and 5am, the violent clanging of the great bell at the Abbey alerted the neighbourhood that something exciting was occurring.

The Hon. Violet Vivian, daughter of Lord and Lady Swansea, was awakened by her pet dog and found clouds of smoke rising from the floor below. After awakening the household, which apparently numbered 20, she and members of the staff brought the steam fire engine owned by the Vivians out into the rear courtyard. The coachman, Albert Anthony, travelled to Swansea in the meantime to alert the fire brigade, which he did at 5.05am at the Oxford Street section house.

Constable Johns, after informing the other stations, assisted in the reining and harnessing of the horses to the manual engine, and departed for the Abbey at 5.15am. The manual engine was driven by Constable Price, accompanied by Inspector Davies, who was in charge, and five other officers.

At the Abbey, the steam fire engine, along with the Vivians' volunteer brigade, which consisted of Hennings the butler, Hancock and Chips the gardeners, Morgan Walters the engineer and other members of staff, including the head of the brigade Captain Surman, had, due to the lack of water at the Abbey, obtained a water supply from the Swiss pond at the top end of the park. The engine had a good head of steam, and two lengths of hose were soon playing jets of water on the great house. The Abbey's steam fire engine had been purchased from Merryweather's of London some seven years previously, and was far superior to the manual engine owned by borough brigade, which required up to 22 men to operate.

When the borough brigade arrived, they were confronted with the usual lack of water. On Captain Colquhoun's orders, a messenger was sent to Reservoir Lane, in Brynmill, and after operating a series of valves at that location, an ample supply of water was forthcoming from hydrants throughout the Abbey grounds. The whole of the surrounding wooded area was illuminated by the blaze, which by now had enveloped the whole of the back portion of the Abbey. Lady Swansea and her daughters, guests, staff and some firemen tried frantically to rescue what furniture and contents they could. The Abbey, which was a stately and impressive structure, had been visited in 1881 by the then Prince and Princess of Wales, was nothing but a mass of flames, which had spread at an alarming and destroying pace. It was not until around 6.30am that the blaze showed signs of abating, after vast quantities of water had been poured upon it.

At daybreak, just after 7am, the blaze was practically subdued, but the destruction wrought in those three hours had been terrific and thorough. In the servants quarters, not a roof remained, and nearly every passage in the whole of the rear part of the Abbey was blocked by huge falls of plaster and smouldering rafters. If a stiff breeze had been blowing, the Abbey would probably have been engulfed. As it was, the kitchens, scullery, boot hall, nursemaid's room, butler's room, pantries, laundry and drying room, along with Violet and Averill Vivian's bedrooms and several sleeping apartments reserved for visitors, were burnt out, with only the bare walls remaining.

The manual engine was still being worked with a will at 9am the following morning, pouring water onto the smouldering debris when flames were seen. It was thought that the origin of the fire was probably in the boot room, and that it could have been caused by overheating of the flues. At 10.30am Inspector Davies gave permission for some of the firemen, who were looking considerably the worse from their arduous and trying experiences, to return to their station in Swansea with the manual engine, leaving Sergeant Edwards and Constable Tucker, (who had served together in the London Fire Brigade before coming to Swansea) along with some other firemen, to assist with the continued damping down of the smouldering debris.

Singleton Abbey was in the county and not within the confines of the Swansea borough, so when Superintendent Thomas from Neath and Inspector Davies from Gowerton arrived, both from the County Constabulary, responsibility for security was handed over to them. They, along with members of the Vivians' Hafod Works, began to remove the burnt-out woodwork and debris. Most of the furniture and contents of the rear portion of the Abbey had been consumed, but a portrait of the late Lord Swansea was found unaffected, still hanging in its position over the fire place, in the room where Miss Vivian had slept.

A *South Wales Daily Post* reporter, who lived near the Abbey, stated that he had been awakened by 'The gasping of the Abbey's steam fire engine, and the wild alarm sounded by the call bell. The conviction that there was something unusual about had forced him out into the dark and frosty morning in hot haste. When he reached the Abbey, a rousing scene was in full play: 'from the rear of the new wing, giant flames

were mounting, higher and higher, lighting up the avenues and the winter foliage.' Mr H.A. Chapman, a local councillor and photographer, was 'nearly as smart with his plates and camera, as the firemen with their engine, and by noon was exhibiting the toned proofs of the remains of the fire in his shop window.' Unfortunately however, some years later Mr Chapman's shop in the High Street in Swansea was affected by a serious fire of its own, and the press reported that 'many historic photographs of Swansea were lost.'

The fire, although subdued, warranted the attendance of some of the borough firemen until the following day.

The following day the local press reported on the fire, and included direct questions about the fire brigade's inadequacy in tackling serious outbreaks of fire. Although the press praised the firemen's efforts, they vilified the Town Council, demanding to know why they allowed the fire brigade to be so ill equipped. The town was worse off in the matter of fire extinguishing appliances than many a good size village, and the press implied that the council attached greater importance to purchasing a dust destructor and providing electric light for the town than the equipping of the fire brigade.

During the whole of that day, Mr Morgan Walters the engineer, Mr Hennings the butler and members of the borough brigade remained at Singleton Abbey. They inspected the devastation, and occasionally brought the hose into play to subdue a minor outbreak. However, in the early hours of 5 February, the borough firemen out at the Abbey were summoned to attend another fire which had broken out in Swansea.

The fire, which occurred less than 24 hours after that at Singleton Abbey, was on the premises of Mr W. Lloyd, boot manufacturer, in Orange Street, Swansea. At the time it was considered disastrous in the extreme. Police Constable Williams, who was on his beat in that district of the town, saw flames shooting up into the air from the rear of Mr Lloyd's premises, and ran in 'hot haste' to alarm the fire brigade at the Goat Street fire brigade station.

The brigade, under the command of Captain Colquhoun and Superintendent Jones, arrived in full force at the scene a little after 3am, with the manual engine. It was soon in working order and the conflict with the fierce and rapidly spreading flames began. It was evident to all that the workshops had been burning for some time, and the flames had a complete mastery. It took three hours before the firemen's incessant labours showed signs of being rewarded, as the flames began to recede. The scene at daylight was one of complete and irredeemable ruin. The workshops that covered a large space on the ground floor contained the remnants of eight or nine valuable machines, utterly destroyed, along with a large quantity of leather which was in stock and tools and utensils used in the manufacture of boots and shoes. All that remained of the building was the charred walls. The cost of the damage was estimated at £3,000, and was fortunately covered by insurance, but the fire left eight or nine employees out of work. The adjoining premises also suffered. Mrs Davies, on the left of the shop, lost her back kitchen, and Mr Richards, a well-known Swansea saddler on the right, lost large quantities of stock leather when the back portion of his shop was destroyed.

The local *South Wales Daily Post* reported an interview that Captain Colquhoun had given to one of their reporters after the fire. When asked about Swansea's need for a steam fire engine, he replied '... decidedly so, I have made recommendations to the Watch Committee, but they have always been received half heartedly.' This provoked numerous letters on the subject, one of which stated that '... it is a bitter commentary on the apathy of Swansea, that a town the size of Briton Ferry was permitted to snap up an engine offered at a sacrifice, because the second largest town in Wales was unequal to the duty of buying it.' To add insult to injury, the local press

reported on 12 February 1896, that the town of Carmarthen had purchased a steam fire engine.

The month of February was becoming an extremely busy time for the Swansea Fire Brigade. Captain Colquhoun had predicted, in an interview following the Singleton Abbey fire, that people should 'look out for another two fires, they invariably come in threes,' and he was proved right. On Saturday 15 February, the brigade received a telephone message from the county police, informing them that a serious fire had broken out at the Ship and Castle, a hotel on the seafront at Mumbles.

The fire was discovered by the landlord, a Mr Parkman, after his wife said that she had heard noises from downstairs. When he investigated, Mr Parkman was confronted with large volumes of smoke, and, wasting no time, he escorted his wife the other residents, six in all, from the building. The time was around 4.30am. Within 10 minutes, the blaze had illuminated the whole area, and even cast a glowing reflection on the waters of the bay opposite, as well as lighting up the huge rocks behind. It was thought to be even larger than the blaze at Singleton Abbey earlier in the month. Men of the Oystermouth District Council, with limited fire-fighting resources, were quickly on the scene and directing their hose on to the burning mass. In the meantime, the Mumbles Coastguard and Yacht Club officials had telephoned for the Swansea fire brigade, which responded with the manual engine, pulled by two horses. Inspector Davies was in charge, and his crew comprised Sergeant Edwards, Constables 87 Davies, 17 Johns and Harris, and they arrived at the scene in under an an hour. With the tide full in, Swansea's manual engine was man handled down an embankment, over shingle, and set into the sea. An unlimited supply of helpers meant that the engine was soon pumping good streams of water on to the burning building, which had become totally enveloped in flames. The brigade soon decided that no good purpose could be achieved by directing their jets on to the hotel, and they concentrated their efforts in saving the adjoining premises, Mr McCauley's outfitters shop on one side and some derelict cottages on the other. The cottages were eventually left to whatever fate befell them. During the fire-fighting operations the Swansea engine had to be removed from the beach, because of the rising tide. Some of the volunteers waded waist deep into the tide to bring the engine out and set it into the Oystermouth Water Works Company's mains, from which there was a good supply. With little or no time wasted, the firemen re-doubled their efforts, and at about 7.30am the flames began to recede, because there was nothing more to be consumed. All that remained of the hotel were the undressed stone walls, which were eventually pulled down by workmen, as they constituted a danger to passing pedestrians and traffic.

On the evening of Friday 28, the brigade were once again in action, when they attended a fire at the East Dock, on board the SS *Missouri*. The firemen battled throughout the night, but at about 7.30am the following morning Inspector Davies boarded the vessel, and found that the fire had spread to the No.2 hold and was still burning fiercely. In order to quell the spread of fire, some workmen took out a side plate from the port side, with a view to sinking the ship, but before they finished their work, the *Missouri* heeled over. A portion of her starboard side went under, and she began taking on water. The situation was now awkward as well as dangerous, and the order to evacuate the ship was given. Fortunately, the influx of water extinguished the fire.

The press coverage of Swansea's fires prompted Messrs Merryweather's of London to write to the Watch Committee, and the letter was read out at the meeting of 3 March 1896. Merryweather's commended the Swansea fire brigade on their efforts and emphasised the good work done by the Merryweather steam engine at the Singleton Abbey fire. They also alluded to the possibility of Swansea Council purchasing a new engine. They could offer Swansea one of their 250 gallons per minute engines, which would be capable of supplying four jets simultaneously, at an exceptional bargain price.

Alderman Harris remarked that the proposal would entail a considerable discussion, and he was of the opinion that it should be adjourned to a future meeting. Alderman Leeder however, in agreeing to the adjournment, stated that he had received a communication from a Mr Kempthorne, clerk to the Neath Local Board and a Mr Pegge, clerk to the Briton Ferry fire brigade. They reported that their brigade had a fire engine which had cost £750 and pumped 350 gallons per minute, and other fire brigade equipment. They had been paying for the engine and fittings by instalments of £105 per year over seven years, and they were prepared to transfer their liability to the Swansea Corporation. Mr Kempthorne's impression was 'that engines did not save lives, it was the fire escape that did that. The fire engine saved the insurance companies, who never paid a penny towards it'. All the documentation would be transferred to the head constable. Mr Kempthorne asked that the Swansea Corporation discuss the matter at their next meeting.

In June 1896, Captain Colquhoun and Sergeant Edwards travelled to the International Fire Exhibition in London, in order to view the various fire engines and equipment on show. They reported their findings to the Watch Committee, with the hope that a purchase, preferably of a steam engine, would be forthcoming.

Swansea's need for a steam fire engine was also voiced in the local press, and it was stated that the Swansea councillors should take seriously the plight of the fire brigade, especially as places such as Llanelli and Briton Ferry were now in possession of steam engines.

During July, a serious fire occurred in Ilfracombe, across the Bristol Channel from Swansea. It resulted in the complete destruction of the town's arcade. An account of the fire was published in the press, which added new vigour to the argument for Swansea obtaining a steam fire engine. A reporter from the *South Wales Daily Post* even interviewed Captain Colquhoun, asking his views on the subject, to which he replied, 'that he was in the progress of compiling a report on the issue, following his and Sergeant Edwards's visit to the International Fire Exhibition, and when completed, it would be presented to the Watch Committee for their perusal.'

Captain Colquhoun's report was, when presented, quite specific about the fire brigade's need for better equipment. Fire escapes were his first concern, and he stated that the ladders now in use, including those that had been positioned about the town, were showing definite signs of rot, which he attributed to the factory smoke that hung over the town. His primary fear was of a serious accident occurring, if a rung broke when a fireman was descending and carrying someone down the escape. He therefore believed that they should be replaced with smaller and lighter escape ladders, that could be managed by a single man, making them easier to convey to the scene of a fire. These, he suggested, should be placed in various locations about the town, including the Morriston district. The cost of these fire escapes would be between £30 and £35 each.

In relation to the purchase of a steam fire engine, Captain Colquhoun used the example of a fire that had occurred at the Steel Works some years earlier to illustrate his point. He noted that on that occasion it had taken a great deal of effort to recruit sufficient men at the scene to operate the handles of the manual engine. If a steam fire engine had been available, that particular difficulty would not have arisen. He went on to say that there were likely to be occasions, just as there had been in the past, when a steam engine would be exceedingly useful, such as a fire at a large department store, like Ben Evans, or a fire where there was a need to pump large volumes of water a great distance, or up hill.

Councillor Skidmore was also interviewed on the subject. He believed that Swansea was adequately equipped to contend with the most serious outbreaks of fire, and that no need for undue expenditure to purchase additional fire brigade appliances or equipment. When asked about what would happen should a fire occur in the workhouse, (the old Mount Pleasant Hospital) which, because of its location halfway up Mount Pleasant Hill, would probably be gutted before the fire brigade could pump water there, the councillor replied that when the Cray scheme (Cray Reservoir) was complete, Swansea would not lack water in any of its districts.

Because of the number of ship fires that had occurred within the port, some councillors raised the question of whether the fire brigade was legally bound to attend them. The Town Clerk replied '…that it is the Council's duty to protect life and property, by providing a Fire Brigade for such eventualities.'

The Swansea fire brigade however, did not attend a serious fire that occurred during the early hours of Thursday 1 September 1896, at the Currant Tree public house (now the West Cross Inn) in the West Cross, a suburb of the Mumbles. The landlord, Mr Hopkins, had been awakened by a choking sensation to find his bedroom filled with dense smoke. Losing no time, he jumped from the window on to a porch roof, and consequently made it to safety. He then procured a ladder, which he placed to a bedroom window, and attempted to save his niece, who by this time was semi-conscious. She was carried down the ladder to safety. Some 30 minutes or so elapsed before neighbours and police brought a reel from the Mumbles District Council and attempted to subdue the flames. Unfortunately, by this time the pub was totally engulfed, and deemed to be beyond saving. Even though a fire plug was in close proximity, the hose was not connected and the fire was left to take its course.

The reason that the borough brigade did not attend was given in an extract from its occurrence book, which was published by the local press. 'A signal Inspector employed on the Midland Railway visited the Goat Street Police Fire Brigade Station at 7am that morning, and reported that the Currant Tree Inn, West Cross was on fire, but he did not believe that there was any need for the Fire Brigade to attend, as the Inn was isolated and almost destroyed when he had left it.' The duty constable informed the fire brigade, which put itself in a state of readiness, but as no further message relating to the fire was received, they did not respond.

Following the great fire at the Singleton Abbey earlier in the year, another serious fire befell the Vivians, when on Wednesday 28 October 1896, the home of Mr Graham Vivian, at Clyne Castle near Blackpill, was the scene of a serious outbreak. The fire was discovered by one of the maids, Miss Annie Williams, who had been awakened by the stifling smoke which had found its way into her bedroom. She immediately alarmed the household, and the chef, Mr Guyot, attempted to subdue the flames with one of the mansion's corridor hand pumps, unfortunately to no avail. In the meantime the footman, Albert Hood, left the castle for Swansea, in order to inform the fire brigade. At approximately 5.25pm the borough brigade, with its manual engine horsed, and under the command of Superintendent Thomas, departed for the scene. PC Cuff was driving, and the crew consisted of Inspector Davies and seven constables. According to the report they arrived 10 minutes later. They were met by an appalling scene, as the whole central wing was well alight. The castle was well-equipped for dealing with outbreaks of fire, with its own manual fire engine (given by Singleton Abbey, when they purchased their steam engine), hose and even hydrants situated within the grounds. Despite all this equipment and the hose manned by the staff and servants, the flames had still engulfed the building. The arrival of the Swansea fire brigade reduced some of the anxiety, and the systematic fighting of the flames by trained personnel and the borough's manual engine soon had a visible effect.

During the course of the firefighting, PC 55 Bounds and PC 51 Evans had a narrow escape when, as they were directing their jets within the castle, the floor collapsed and hurled them into the burning mass below. Although great alarm and terror prevailed for a moment, happily the men were extricated by their colleagues. PC Evans sustained no more than serious shock, although PC Bounds, had a nasty gash across his head.

Both manuals had worked throughout, and at around 8.30am the fire began to show signs of abating, and the firemen were able to slacken their efforts. Captain Colquhoun, who had arrived at the castle on horseback a little while after the brigade, had been directing operations throughout. He decided that the attendance of the fire brigade was still required, as a keen eye for sectional outbreaks was needed. The fire was eventually extinguished at around 11.45am and the firemen returned to Swansea at 1.30pm.

Mr Graham Vivian praised the Swansea brigade for the manner and rapidity in which they extinguished the blaze, when he stated: 'Never was a big fire better handled.' The excitement and confusion of the outbreak had meant that no message had been conveyed to Singleton Abbey, so their steam fire engine had not attended the fire.

It was believed that the fire had originated from clothes coming into contact with a spark from one of the fires in the state bedroom of the centre wing. Within the castle were several priceless antiques, some of which were completely destroyed, including a cabinet that housed a complete set of Swansea china, valued at the time at around £25,000. Mr Graham Vivian's most treasured possessions, which were considered priceless as well as being regarded as one of the finest examples of mediaeval art, were the tapestries that adorned the walls of the castle. These, thankfully, were saved, and their intrinsic value was considered at the time to exceed that of the whole castle and its contents.

In December, following a fire on board a barge laden with pitch, Captain Colquhoun informed the Watch Committee that he had presented a bill for the expenses incurred by the fire brigade to Mr Law, superintendent of the Harbour Trust. The bill was for the employment of 39 men to operate the manual, and their refreshments. The manual required 20 men to operate it plus reliefs, and as they had been required to pump hard for quite a while, the amount incurred was £5 14s. Captain Colquhoun further stated that the Harbour Trust had refused to pay the bill, claiming that they were entitled to the same services as other ratepayers.

This report by Captain Colquhoun fuelled old arguments about payments for expenses incurred by the fire brigade while attending fires. Councillor Leeder proposed that the Harbour Trust should be contacted with the view to arranging for payments for services in regard to fires on insured vessels within the port.

1896 had been an extremely busy time for the Swansea fire brigade, with many serious fires. The brigade, however, had acquitted itself admirably, and many compliments and commendations had been expressed in the local press.

After Captain Colquhoun's report in July 1896 about the replacement of the fire escapes, which were in poor condition, he conducted a survey around the town in January 1897 to establish the height of buildings and the height of escapes required to reach them. Two of Swansea's highest buildings, the Ben Evans department store and the Grand Hotel, were singled out and an escape was taken along for testing purposes. Captain Colquhoun ascertained that an escape 60ft high would be required. Because of the size of these larger escapes, it was suggested that they should be positioned around the town at specially chosen locations.

Captain Colquhoun, in his November report to the Watch Committee, reiterated that there was now an urgent need for the escapes to be replaced. If an accident occurred he would not be held responsible. Four escapes were now required, and he recommended that following their purchase they be placed at the various police stations. The committee agreed to purchase two escapes at a cost of £180 each, placing one at the hospital and the other in Morriston.

In July 1897, Messrs William Rose exhibited their fire escape ladders at the Guildhall, and Captain Colquhoun and Superintendent Thomas, with other members of the brigade, attended. A demonstration took place to display the new Kingston fire escape with its integral hose cart. The escape's inventor, Mr George Melvin, along with a contingent of councillors, oversaw proceedings. The Kingston escape contended with the brigade's Shand Mason escape, and with the demonstration completed, the committee agreed to the purchase of two of the Messrs Rose escapes, at a cost of £90 each.

On a lighter note, Sergeant Edwards, in February 1898, requested permission to organise a fire brigade dinner. He hoped this would become an annual event. Although permission was granted by the committee, it was on the understanding that the brigade members would wear their uniforms and the pump would be placed nearby in the event of an outbreak of fire occurring. The local press reported that many guests had been invited, and the chief guest was Captain Scott, of the Llanelli fire brigade. During his speech he traded compliments with Captain Colquhoun, and they promised to assist each other should the need arise.

The promise to assist each other made at the annual dinner was called in on Saturday 12 March 1898. At Captain Scott's request, the Swansea fire brigade responded to a fire at the coal tips in Tumble, near Llanelli. The fire had spread in the direction of an engine house at the colliery, which if ignited would have terrible consequences to a nearby row of houses and two hotels. According to a report, the two brigades performed admirably and contained the outbreak.

The purchase of a steam fire engine was once more considered unnecessary when it was again discussed at the January 1899 committee meeting. The reason given was that the town's mains and water pressure were more than adequate for dealing with any outbreak of fire. It was at this time that Inspector Davies announced his retirement. He had been a prominent member of the Swansea fire brigade, and now, after nearly 30 years, he retired on superannuation (pension) of 73s 4d per week, plus 1s per week fire brigade pension.

Not since 1896 had Swansea had to contend with a serious outbreak of fire, when at just after 2am on Tuesday 9 May 1899, the Hotel Metropole in Wind Street became the scene of a disastrous and costly fire. The hotel, which was in the final stages of construction, incurred damages estimated at £4,000–£5,000.

The fire was discovered by a man named Biddle, who reported it to the nearby Guildhall police station. They in turn informed the other fire brigade stations at High Street, Goat Street and the Oxford Street section house, all of whom responded with the relevant engines and equipment, arriving at the scene a little after 2.30am. Within a few minutes they were reported to have had their hoses charged and playing upon the flames, which at the time seemed to be confined to the upper bedrooms of the east wing, at the rear of the hotel. The firemen were experiencing difficulties in approaching the flames, because they did not know the layout of the hotel interior. The flames by this time seemed to envelope the whole building, as well as the adjoining property of the Conservative Club. A report stated that Captain Colquhoun was in charge, with Superintendent Thomas, Inspector Evans, three sergeants and 14 constables, all of whom worked feverishly, but whose combined efforts seemed to produce feeble results. The glare from the blaze could be seen from all around the town for three hours or more. At the rear of the hotel there was a winter garden, which was covered by a large glass roof. During the fire this roof collapsed, with what was described as a 'deafening thundering crash'.

The firemen, who on this occasion had a powerful and constant supply of water, saw the fruits of their labour when at around 7am the blaze was finally extinguished.

Although the firemen at the Metropole Hotel had a constant and ample supply of water throughout, the Swansea Corporation was publicly condemned after a fire on 10 May, at the Graigola fuel works. The works had expended vast amounts of money installing fire plugs, hydrants and hoses throughout the works, so that their workmen would be able to subdue any fire before the attendance of the fire brigade was required. However, the Corporation's policy at this time was to turn the water supply off at night, for as much as eight hours, and this rendered the works' water main and apparatus useless. It was reported that 'despite the money spent on appliances for dealing with fire, was rendered as helpless, as if the works had been outside the Borough, and no provision whatever had been made.' Fortunately the fire was detected in its early stages by the works storekeeper, and as the canal was close by, the fire was eventually extinguished by the use of a bucket chain.

In June 1899 an article appeared in the local press about Swansea's recent fires, commenting on the town's inability to provide the necessary precautions for dealing with outbreaks of fire. It went on to state that the town still did not possess a steam fire engine, unlike some of its small neighbouring towns, and persisted in its policy of turning off the water supply at night. At the Metropole Hotel fire, where a good supply was forthcoming, it was at the expense of turning off or diverting the water from other parts of town, a practice which could have had disastrous results at the recent Graigola fuel works fire.

Just after 1am on Tuesday 12 June, a constable walking his beat in the vicinity of the Swansea market responded to cries of 'Fire!'. He found that the market was well ablaze, and the fire brigade had already been alerted. Sergeant Edwards and a crew of four constables responded from the Goat Street station, but on their arrival they were confronted by the whole of the central span of the market burning fiercely. Standpipes were set into hydrants in Orange Street and Union Street, and jets were soon playing on the structure. The firefighters were soon joined by a Oxford Street section house contingent, who immediately set their hoses into the Oxford Street main, close to the market entrance.

Under the direction of Captain Colquhoun and Superintendent Thomas, the firemen's jets were soon having the desired effect, and the outbreak was brought under control at around 4am. The fire brigade contingent, including the captain and superintendent, amounted to over 20 personnel. The origin of the outbreak was unknown, but this did not stop conjecture. The cause was thought to be the heat of the sun through the glass on to matches in one of the stalls, rats gnawing through an electric wire, discarded cigarettes, or even possible arson. The council accepted an offer of £3,637 10s from the insurance company for the damage sustained.

In Westminster, on 5 July 1899, the Fire Brigades Committee of the House of Commons met. The meeting was presided over by Mr Jesse Collins, and evidence was given about fire protection in South Wales and fire appliances. The author of the bill was Mr Guy Pym MP, a member of the committee who had reported on his deliberations following reports issued to him by Clerks of the various councils in South Wales.

It was stated that there were 21 urban district councils, 9 rural district councils and 69 parish councils. Within these councils there were only fire appliances for 14 brigades, and there were seven urban district councils without a fire brigade at all.

Swansea, it was reported, possessed four manual fire engines, but no steam engine. This was considered an important point. Swansea's geographical area meant that water mains in the town boasted a pressure of 60 pounds, but this was considerably less in other parts of the borough. The situation was thought to be unacceptable, as a pressure of 75 pounds was ideal. The Swansea brigade, however, recognised their deficiencies and had asked the council to supply them with a steam engine and a large escape ladder.

Swansea in the meantime had been granted a local government board loan of £450 to increase the water supply in the High Street, and was also recommended to install valve hydrants in preference to the ball hydrants.

Captain Scott, of the neighbouring Llanelli fire brigade, was also secretary of the National Fire Brigades Union for South Wales, and he stated that his brigade was under the supervision of the district council, which considered that there was a good supply of water within the town, with sufficient pressure. They had two stations, one possessing a steam fire engine, two hose carts, 1,500ft of hose and a fire escape. The other station possessed a hose cart, with 350ft of hose, and two ladders were positioned in the town. The fire brigade consisted of one officer, one second officer, one engineer, 13 firemen and three boy messengers, and a local horse keeper supplied horses for the Brigade.

In October 1899, Captain Colquhoun recommended that the council purchase the site of the old Ragged School, which he believed was a good location for the erection of a new central police fire brigade station, at an estimated cost of £9,000.

Chapter Five

The Beginning of a New Century

Swansea in the 1800s had seen some remarkable achievements. Originally a town with no fire brigade, in 1836 the emergence of the 'Fire Bobby' led to the police being given overall responsibility for the town's firefighting, a duty which they carried out until 1941, with a break of just four years, 1858–1862. Under Head Constable John Allison, the brigade had seen dramatic times, including the Temple Street fire. When Mr Allison retired prematurely, Swansea saw the arrival of Captain Colquhoun, and under his leadership and command the Swansea fire brigade gained much praise and admiration. Now, at the beginning of a new century, Swansea was to see the long awaited arrival of a steam fire engine, then motorisation and World War One. During the war the brigade struggled as its experienced personnel joined the forces. The police and fire brigade were augmented by 'specials' until the creation of the Auxiliary Fire Service (AFS) in 1938 after a Fire Service Act. The National Fire Service (NFS) was formed in August 1941, and remained until a Government Act in 1947 handed over responsibility for the fire brigades to the relevant local authorities, a change affected in April 1948. In Swansea this meant a fire brigade totally devoid of police responsibility. Also in the 1900s, on a more tragic note, Swansea would experience the deaths of firemen.

In April 1900 a report was printed regarding the proposed erection of a new central fire station, which would be situated at the rear of the Alexandra Road Free Library, abutting on to Pleasant Street. The site had been previously mentioned by Captain Colquhoun, and the proposed cost of the new station was £10,000–£12,000.

The borough surveyor was instructed to draw up the necessary plans for the Watch Committee's approval. Although the cost of the new station was high, it was proposed that it should replace the Guildhall, High Street, Goat Street and Oxford Street stations.

The head constable, in his monthly report in October 1900, said that he favoured the library site for the proposed new central station. The current situation, with the brigade and its fire appliances divided between the four different stations, meant that he thought that he and the brigade could not be held responsible for any delays in arriving at fires. The mayor remarked that if new stations were erected, and the brigade's response quickened, then the insurance companies would benefit. He therefore considered that the various insurance companies should be contacted and asked to contribute to the cost of the new station.

In December, the borough surveyor produced the plans for the new central police fire brigade station, on the site at the rear of the Alexandra Road Free Library. Unfortunately the site in question was partly occupied by the old Ragged School, and he suggested that the council contact the trustees of the school to suggest a new site for the school. There was a potential plot opposite, on the corner of Pleasant Street and Richard Street. This would allow the current building to be demolished to make way for the new station.

The new century began a great deal quieter than the old one had finished, and the borough brigade only had to deal with comparatively small fires. What seems to have been the first more serious blaze of the century occurred in July 1901, near the New Cut Bridge in the St Thomas district. The fire broke out on the premises of two lock-up shops, owned by Mr Paton and Mr Huxtable, at around midnight. Fortunately, a good supply of water was available, and the report stated that without the efficiency of the fire brigade, under the command of Captain Colquhoun, the fire would have been far more devastating. At the height of the fire the brigade officers present included Inspector Evans, Sergeant Edwards and 21 constables, who were admirably assisted by a contingent from the Weaver's works brigade, who were in possession of a steam fire engine, and the Midland Railway fire brigade.

On 25 September 1901, an article appeared in the *South Wales Daily Post* about the history of the Swansea fire brigade under the leadership of Captain Colquhoun. The article was taken from a report that had been published in a Cardiff newspaper, and was basically a tribute to Captain Colquhoun.

In the early hours of Tuesday 25 November 1901, a fire broke out on board the SS *Fern*, which was lying in the Prince of Wales Dock. The fire involved sleepers that had been soaked in creosote, and the

brigade, consisting of Sergeant Edwards and 13 constables, responded with the usual apparatus and manual engine. The firemen were seriously hampered by the intense heat and smoke, indeed the heat was so fierce that it buckled the ship's sides. The outbreak took nearly four hours to subdue, and the ship took on a list towards the quay wall under the weight of the water that had been poured onto the flames. The brigade remained to damp down the smouldering cargo until 11am. The fire, however, had been accompanied by tragedy. During the blaze the ropes of a derrick had been burnt through, and it collapsed on to a young man, killing him instantly. The dead man was named as Thomas Lewis, aged 24, from Danygraig Road in St Thomas. He had been helping to extinguish the flames.

On Sunday 15 December 1901, the Swansea brigade was summoned to attend a serious fire that had occurred in the main street of Ystalyfera, nearly 13 miles from Swansea. The brigade had received the call at around 3.40am and responded in the usual fashion. With Sergeant Edwards in charge, and a crew consisting of PC 17 Johns, PC 34 Jones, PC 44 Howard and PC 81 Bowen, they arrived at the scene shortly after 5am. On arrival they were confronted by a fire involving a shop, and two adjoining houses and a public house. Their first difficulty was that there was no water supply, and there were no hydrants or firefighting appliances in the district. The road was torn up in order to locate the main, under the supervision of William Morgan, who was employed by the local council. With a water supply established, the Swansea brigade fought the fire, which by then had totally engulfed Shepherd's shop and the two adjoining houses and caused serious damage to the Red Cow public house. At one time it was feared that the whole block of six shops would be destroyed, but fortunately the brigade were successful in preventing the fire from spreading. The fire was practically extinguished by around 11am, and the brigade returned to Swansea at 1.50pm. After the fire a haulier named Firman, employed by Mr Shepherd, was charged with arson.

A fire which was described as 'a great fire in Landore' occurred at 4am on Wednesday 8 January 1902, at the Tin Stamping Works, Landore, near the low-level railway station. Men from the local station were first at the scene with their hand cart and hose, and they set into the nearest main. The Morriston and Swansea stations were contacted and a Morriston contingent arrived shortly after, with another hose. There was concern that the Swansea brigade had not arrived, until word was passed that they had been involved in an accident en route. The Swansea engine, under the command of Superintendent Thomas and carrying seven constables, had got just past the junction of Prince of Wales Road and Bridge Street in the Hafod, when one of the rear wheels got caught in a tram line. This broke the axle and wrenched off the rear wheel, and all the crew were thrown into the roadway. The driver was able to hold on to the horses and stop them from bolting. Unfortunately, Constables Bowen and Howard needed hospital treatment for minor injuries. The damaged engine was pushed into the side of the road and the remaining constables continued to the fire on foot, arriving at around 5am when the fire was at its height. Men from all three brigade stations remained at the scene throughout the night and late into the morning, when the true extent of the damage could be seen. The damage was estimated at £5,000.

A rescue by PC Tucker, must go down in the annals of the Swansea fire brigade's history as one of the most extraordinary and heroic acts by a fireman. There was a fire place in a drapers shop in the High Street a little after 3am on Friday 6 February 1902. The brigade, although they arrived promptly at the scene, discovered that the premises were well alight, and thick volumes of smoke were issuing from the building. The men were immediately informed that six people were asleep inside. PC Tucker, with no

Police Fireman Thomas 'Tommy' Tucker, who was decorated on two occasions. The first was for a rescue in Tontine Street, Swansea, on 22 September 1893, for which he was awarded the Quiver Medal. The second rescue, for which he was awarded the Royal Society for the Protection of Life from Fire Medal, took place at a draper's shop next door to the Ty Melyn public house in the High Street, Swansea, on 6 February 1902. (Mrs Enid John and Alan Gower)

thought for his personal safety, ran into the building and ascended the stairs. He directed the residents to keep their heads at the windows, away from the smoke, until he was able to retrieve and tie some bed sheets together. Using this make-shift rope he lowered the residents one by one on to a lower roof, from where they could enter the adjoining premises of the Ty Melyn public house. He then carried a child out of the building on his back and emerged through

Tommy Tucker's medals. The Quiver Medal (left) was awarded by newspapers in recognition of outstanding bravery. The other medal is the Royal Society for the Protection of Life from Fire Medal.

the front of the Ty Melyn to applause from the crowd of people that had gathered.

While PC Tucker was effecting his rescues, the remainder of the brigade were busy preventing the flames from spreading to the rest of the block, as the flames were rising well into the air. They were successful in their task, and confined the fire to Mr Chavenson's drapers.

At the next Watch Committee meeting PC Tucker was commended for his bravery and awarded a gratuity of £5 by the council. He was also awarded the medal of the Royal Humane Society for the Preservation of Life from Fire.

The local press reported that although Swansea had its own hero in PC Tucker, the London Fire Brigade had its own similar hero. A fireman by the name of T. Bartlett, son-in-law of Mr Beer, a contractor in the Strand, Swansea, had been instrumental in rescuing nine people from a fire in Air Street, Piccadilly in London.

In September, a fire which was described as 'disastrous' occurred in the upper High Street, resulting in the destruction of three properties, that of Mr Jabex Davies, provision merchant, a fried fish shop next door and a pickling and storage house belonging to Mr Morgan, a butcher. The fire was believed to have originated in the office of the provision merchant's premises, and quickly spread throughout. The fire brigade, despite their usual promptness, experienced difficulties in obtaining water due to the non-arrival of the turncock. Some 15 minutes elapsed before a good supply could be established, then standpipes were set into Jockey Street, Matthew Street and the High Street, so jets could be played on the burning buildings. Swansea's practice of turning off the water supply was once again condemned in the local press, and it was suggested that the police could act as turncocks in the event of a fire. Captain Colquhoun totally rejected this idea, as he believed, as he always had, that the valve system for diverting water was too complex for police to be trained to operate on an occasional basis.

As a result of this latest fire, Captain Colquhoun formulated a report for the Watch Committee about the fire brigade's appliances. The main reason for the delay was that the alarm bell for the turncock's telephone had not rung, so the first the turncock had heard of the fire was when a messenger arrived at his house to inform him. Captain Colquhoun told the meeting that when a new central station was erected, there should be ample space for accommodating all the fire brigade's appliances. Until an adequate supply of water could be maintained, day or night, his plans did not include the purchase of steam fire engine.

Delays due to defective telephone equipment continued to afflict the fire brigade, as breakdowns in communication between stations and with the turncock were experienced and became more common. This was a result of the fact that the system had not been overhauled, as it was thought that

Opposite page:
Bedsheets hanging from an upstairs window at the scene of the draper's shop fire, next to the Ty Melyn public house in 1902. (Mrs Enid John)

maintenance would be done when the system was reinstalled in the as yet unbuilt new central station.

An eyewitness at the fire in the High Street remarked in the local press: '…the fire in High Street should be a lesson to the town. Why cannot we get a fire engine? Has the town become so poor that it cannot afford one? We want, I should say two, fire is a good friend, but a bad enemy. Let the ratepayers lock together and compel the Council to buy one.'

Much indignation was expressed by the inhabitants of Rhondda Street, in the Mount Pleasant district of Swansea, when, at a serious fire at No. 83 on 20 February 1903, there was no water, as the supply was cut off. It was reported that Sergeant Edwards and the firemen were pacing up and down the street, with the hose run out and lying at their feet, waiting for a supply for nearly 40 minutes. The fire had taken a complete hold of the premises, leaving the firemen, when water was finally obtained, no option but to concentrate their efforts on saving the adjoining houses, Nos 81 and 85. This, however, was no easy task, as although there was a water supply, the pressure was so poor that it would not reach the eaves of the houses. A ladder was procured and it was reported that a nimble fireman ascended to the roof and directed some water on to the flames. Little as it was, he broke through the slates with his axe. When a good supply at sufficient force became available, the brigade were able to subdue the flames at the doomed No.83, thereby saving the adjoining houses.

To add insult to injury, following the fire it was reported that the Mount Pleasant police sub-station had been unable to contact the Goat Street fire brigade station as they could not obtain a signal. This was attributed to the ongoing faults with the police telephone system. Before the fire brigade could be alerted, a messenger had to be sent to the workhouse (Mount Pleasant Hospital), whereby the fire brigade were informed by the national telephone system.

After the Rhondda Street fire, the local press published letters from the concerned public, all of which condemned the defective water supply and telephone system, and urged the council to remedy the situation by urgently concluding the Cray Reservoir scheme, along with the erection of the new police and fire brigade station and the purchase of new fire appliances for the town.

Whether as a result of public pressure or not, the Swansea General Purposes Committee, on 11 March 1903, adopted the tender of Mr John Williams, builder, for the erection of a new police fire brigade station in Pleasant Street, at the rear of the Alexandra Road Library.

The *South Wales Daily Post*, on 24 April 1903, reported that PC 17 Johns had passed away. Although he had been on duty as recently as the previous Wednesday, PC Johns had been involved in an accident involving the brigade's manual engine and a cart. On 16 April, when the brigade were turning out to sleepers on fire at the East Dock, the manual collided with the grocery cart of Mr David Morgan of Llansamlet while negotiating a bend near the Rhondda and Swansea Bay railway bridge. The nature of the injuries that led to PC Johns's death was not reported.

The question of the defective police telephone system arose again when, at a fire at Cwmbwrla on Saturday 27 February 1904, a constable was unable to alert the fire brigade. He was forced to run from Cwmbwrla to the High Street police station to raise the alarm. Possibly as a result of this delay, the house was totally engulfed, and the blind occupant, Mr Charles White, perished in the blaze. As a result of the tragedy, a hose cart and escape ladder were purchased for the Cwmbwrla district.

The annual Bath & West Agricultural Show visited Swansea's Victoria Park, where, as on previous occasions, Merryweather's provided the fire cover. This afforded the famous London fire engine manufacturer the opportunity to display their latest fire appliances. Looking at Swansea as a potential customer, they displayed their 'Fire King' motor steam fire engine, along with their horse-drawn 'Greenwich Gem' steam fire engine. The 'Fire King' was a steam-driven mounted pump on a motorised chassis, advertised as able to travel at 30mph and negotiate hills of a gradient up to 1 in 6. This and the 350gpm 'Greenwich Gem' horse-drawn steamer were put through their paces in a display for Captain Colquhoun and the Watch Committee at the Guildhall. The demonstration was carried out under the personal supervision of the principal of Merryweather's, and impressed all who witnessed the display. After the demonstration, the motor fire engine went on a test drive around the town, with Captain Colquhoun as a guest passenger.

The Swansea police fire brigade station, erected in 1905 in Pleasant Street and pictured on an old Swansea postcard.

The Merryweather demonstration had impressed all those present on the day, but the same could not be said of Swansea's fire appliances. The following month, Captain Colquhoun supervised the fire brigade at a simulated fire at the Ben Evans store. Five jets, all supplied from hydrants, were positioned at different locations around the store, but were limited in effect by poor pressure. At the conclusion of the test Captain Colquhoun said that even if the town did purchase a steamer, there would not be sufficient water to supply it. In addition, the hose was in such poor condition that it would not be able to take the pressure.

This exercise by Captain Colquhoun brought the question of Swansea's protection against fire to the fore once more. As major concerns were voiced, the test proved the ineffectiveness of the town's capabilities in dealing with fire. The supply in the vicinity of the Ben Evans store was a 12-inch main, with possibly the best pressure attainable in the borough, but even with this, a jet was unable to extend over the store. The jets barely reached the top floor even when a more forceful supply was obtained after the turncock directed the supply from the Townhill Reservoir, some 300ft above sea level. Both the hose and the town's mains were inadequate, as a higher pressure proved too great for them and resulted in some bursts.

In December 1904, Sergeant Edwards was promoted to Inspector of the fire brigade, and Constable Howard was promoted to sergeant. This added 3s per week to his fire brigade pay.

Swansea was reported at one time to have had four manual engines, but whether they were defective or obsolete is unclear. On most occasions fires were attended with hand carts, and the hose used directly from hydrants. In March 1905, a Great Western Railway official was alerted to a fire at the Danygraig engine sheds. He in turn informed the Swansea fire brigade, only to be told that their engine was 'out of repair' and had been so for two weeks. The Corporation, which had apparently undertaken to do the repairs, was held responsible for the delay. It was reported that the Corporation smith, when asked about the delay in the engine's repair, replied that he had 'more important work to do'. Also in March, as a result of a serious fire at the Swansea Market, the local press concluded:

> Considerable comment has been excited by the fact, that within a short space of 96 hours, two fires of such formidable possibilities should have occurred, when the towns 'only fire engine' should have been under repair.

With the borough brigade still without its engine,

a fire resulting in £20,000-worth of damage occurred at the premises of Parry & Rocke, skin, hide and woollen merchants, in the Strand. The fire, which started just before 5.30am on 29 March 1905, totally engulfed the building, resulting in the collapse of the roof, floors and even parts of the walls. Debris falling from the walls inflicted severe damage on the hose, and fireman working nearby were in danger of being hit. Swansea, having enjoyed complete immunity from serious fires for a considerable period, had suffered four outbreaks in a week, three of them involving the destruction of property on an extensive scale. The total estimated damage caused by the fires at the Danygraig engine sheds, Anderson & Cox, Swansea market and Parry & Rocke, was £35,000.

The April meeting of the Watch Committee asked, as a result of the latest epidemic of fires in Swansea, about the capability of the town's fire brigade to deal with further fires in the borough. Captain Colquhoun informed them that the manual engine was still not available, as it required painting. He also remarked that if the manual had been available at the Parry & Rocke fire in the Strand, it would have required 48 men to work it. This led some councillors to suggest that perhaps now was time to purchase a steam engine. The meeting approved the promotion to superintendent of Inspector Gill, which in effect made him deputy head constable.

The four fires had a long-awaited effect on the Watch Committee, which, in April 1905, finally recommended the purchase of a steam engine. This would at last provide the brigade with an efficient and up-to-date appliance. However, the new police fire brigade station, which was being built in Pleasant Street, was criticised. It was thought that there would be difficulty in manoeuvring the engine out of the station into the narrow lane, and in housing the steam engine within the building. There was only provision for stabling two horses at the new station, but a steam engine, due to its weight, and the distances and gradients in the borough, would require four horses to pull it. There was also concern about the fact that three of the four fires had occurred in the town centre, where there was a reasonable supply and pressure, whereas outside the town centre conditions were less favourable. The committee finally recommended that specifications for a steam fire engine be forwarded to Merryweather's and Shand Mason. In May the council recommended the purchase of a steam fire engine from Messrs Shand Mason at a cost of £330.

Swansea's new central police fire brigade station was also in the headlines: 'Swansea's new Police and Fire Brigade Station, bad designing' and 'inconveniently and dangerously situated.' These remarks had obviously come about after the statements made at the Watch Committee meeting about the narrowness of the appliance room door and the lack of stable space. The new station's design failings could be attributed to the fact that the original plot of ground allocated to the building was nearly double the size of the plot it had in fact been constructed on. The size had been reduced by the Property Committee.

The new central police fire brigade station was opened on Friday 20 July 1905. It had cost an estimated £8,000. Due to the adverse criticism it had received during its erection, it was not formally opened, and the possessions and equipment were transferred to it by members of the force. The opening of the new station meant that the Goat Street and High Street stations were closed. The Local Government Board also sanctioned a loan of £330, in lieu of payment for the steam fire engine. The council leased premises at Gwydr Crescent, Uplands, 1–2 Harcourt Street Mount Pleasant, 1–2 Cwm Level Road Brynhyfryd, and 25 Edward Street (now Iorwerth St.) Manselton, as district police and fire brigade stations.

The long-awaited arrival of Swansea's Shand Mason steam fire engine came in February 1906, when it was eventually delivered. The local *South*

Swansea police fire brigade at the Pleasant Street fire station in 1906. Seated with his dog Jack is Inspector John George Edwards, superintendent of the brigade. To his left is Deputy Chief Constable Gill. (Swansea fire brigade)

Wales Daily Post newspaper reported that before a crowd of some 'two thousand' people, Inspector Edwards and a dozen of his men tested the new arrival. The steamer, which was put through its paces for Captain Colquhoun and members of the council at the Ben Evans store, Castle Street. All were suitably impressed with their new possession. With a good head of steam generated, it projected a continuous stream of water a great height, well over the tower and its flagstaff.

In July, the brigade's steam engine responded to a fire call at Baldwin's Works in Plasmarl. Three of the firemen travelled to the scene of the fire in a tramcar, and returned by landau.

The Co-operative Store in Pontardulais, approximately nine miles from Swansea, was, in the early hours of 23 January 1908, the scene of a serious fire, which was described as a 'glowing furnace.' Although Pontardulais had a 'fire brigade' at the time, it comprised of local constables, who in the event of a fire were assisted by volunteers and supported by a Merryweather manual engine owned by the parish council. The local firefighters were unfortunately no match for the inferno. There were no fire hydrants, and there was also a deficiency in the hose. A telephone message requested the assistance of the Swansea brigade, which call was received at 1.55am. Following the procurement of horses from Bullin's

stables, the steamer, pulled by four horses, was crewed by Inspector Edwards and Constables W. Bounds, Thorne, Kennedy, Goad and Evans. Their arrival at the scene, at approximately 2.45am, was heralded with shouts and cheers from all those present. The fire by this time had reached alarming proportions, as it was virtually unchecked it had spread to the adjoining premises, leaving the brigade the only option of attempting to contain it in those buildings already consumed. The fire had totally destroyed the Co-operative Store and severely damaged two adjoining shops. The ruins continued smouldering for almost a week, and were attended for damping down purposes by the local police, Sergeant German and PCs Lloyd and Owen.

After the Pontardulais fire, the Swansea Watch Committee discussed again the town brigade's attendance at fires in 'outside districts', only to conclude that, prior to the brigade responding, assurances had to be gained from those requesting assistance that they were responsible for meeting the brigade's expenses. The committee believed that the neighbouring district authorities should enter into an agreement with the Swansea Corporation, to alleviate delays in the brigade's attendance at fires. Apparently, there had been a delay of around five minutes in the Swansea brigade responding to the Pontardulais fire, as the secretary of the Co-operative Store had to be contacted to accept that the Store would meet the brigade's expenses.

The following month, the Swansea Brigade once again had to seek assurances for payment before responding to a call-out. At around 9pm on 28 February, an alarm was received informing the fire brigade of a serious fire at Western Grange, on Bishopston Common, some six miles west of Swansea. With a strong wind blowing, which fanned the flames, the house was totally engulfed before the arrival of the Swansea brigade. Initially the brigade were hampered by the lack of water, as the only supplies were obtainable from nearby wells. This necessitated the re-location of the steam engine to adjacent wells once a well had become exhausted.

The discussion about payment for Swansea's fire brigade while attending fires in outlying districts continued, and even included the insurance companies. The Swansea council favoured an annual rate from the outlying authorities, which was acceptable to some, but others were unsure. As a result, the insurance companies were consulted, and they were prepared to entertain claims for the services of the Swansea brigade while attending fires in outlying districts, but would only pay a proportion of the costs applicable to properties covered by them.

In September 1908, around 30 representatives from outlying district authorities met the Swansea Corporation in an attempt to resolve the discussion about payments for the Swansea brigade. The lack of records of this meeting suggests that, like many other meetings, it ended with no decision taken.

With the issue still unresolved, the brigade, on 13 November 1908, were called to a fire that took them on a 40-mile round trip. The call came at 9.15pm, requesting their assistance at the Glanamman Tin Plate Works. The steamer, under the command of Inspector Edwards and his crew, was brought out, and set off on a journey that took around two hours. They eventually returned at 4am the following morning.

The fire brigade, in April 1909, were requested to attend a fire at the Hafod Copper Works, but they were unable to respond with their usual alacrity. The prison van was out with the brigade's horses, but some officers, with presence of mind, seconded the motor ambulance (the police were responsible for the town's ambulance service at the time). They

Opposite page:
Swansea Police fire brigade posing with their new acquisition, a Shand Mason steam fire engine, in February 1906. Inspector Edwards, on the left of the photograph, has Deputy Chief Constable Gill on his left. At the base of the ladder is Sergeant Bounds. (Swansea Reference Library)

equipped it with standpipes and hose, and attended the fire, so that by the time the steamer arrived on the scene the standpipes and hose were already in readiness.

Also in April, since it was still unclear whether or not the Swansea brigade would attend fires outside the borough, the Pontardulais Parish Council decided to form a volunteer fire brigade. Several members were enrolled and new equipment was purchased, and it was decided that Inspector Edwards of the borough brigade would train the potential firemen. In the event of a fire, a siren situated on the Cambrian Tin Plate Works would be sounded.

In May 1909, a fire started at 11am which was to develop into one of Swansea's greatest. The fire took hold on the town side of the South Dock near the Glasgow Wharf, at Glassbrook's timber yard. An onlooker at the wharf said

> …that the fire had started between the Glasgow Wharf and Glassbrook's Timber Yard, the start of the outbreak was as dramatic and unexpected as the fury with which it burned. Fanned by a light wind, blowing to the westward, both the timber yard and the wharf were soon a mass of flames, and by the time the Fire Brigade arrived, which could only have been about 15 minutes, the wharf was wrapped in a blazing mantle, while the smoke from the timber yard was driving over the bottom of Wind Street in dense black clouds. The Brigade were to set the manual to work in Gloucester Place, while the steamer was set into the South Dock, near the lock gates, then, with a good supply of water, they set about their task.

The chief efforts of the firemen, who were working in scorching heat which could be felt 50 yards away, were directed toward preventing the spread of the fire to the Corporation Store and further down the timber yard, toward Pocketts Wharf.

Within half an hour Corker & Bevan's Hay Store was completely demolished. The lower end of the timber yard had caught fire, together with the rear of the Custom House, and the Gloucester Buildings block was also threatened. The upper part of the timber yard was doomed, and the Corporation yard store, in which there was a large quantity of wood paving blocks, and Pocketts Wharf were also threatened. The timber yard was still burning furiously at 1pm, even though the firemen had worked tirelessly. Their efforts, although accompanied by copious streams of water, did not have the desired effect. Remarkably however, the sheds at Pocketts Wharf escaped the flames. Just as the flames seemed certain to spread to the sheds, the wind veered, and only the corner of Glasgow Wharf suffered. The Custom House also had a narrow escape, and only the rooms at the rear of the ground floor were badly damaged by heat and water.

At 3pm that afternoon, the fire was deemed to be under control. It was confined to the Gloucester Place end of the timber yard, and no other premises were in danger. The total damage done by the fire was estimated at between £25,000 and £30,000, and the firemen remained at the scene until midnight. During the fire, the borough brigade were assisted by the Graigola Works Fire Brigade, with their dozen men and equipment, as well as by the docks police.

The press, following the fire, reported that 'the fire engine (steamer) did admirable work, sending forth volumes of water, by means of four lengths of hose, from its location at the South Dock.' Also, a general opinion was voiced that Swansea should have a larger fire brigade. The press further reported that

> …Tuesday 11 May 1909 will go on record as the most fiery in the history of Swansea. At the turn of midnight, there had been an outbreak at the stables of

Messrs Alsopps and Co. Victoria Road, in which five valuable horses perished, then at 11 o'clock that morning, the biggest fire ever seen in the Borough was raging in the vicinity of the South Dock, and still later that day, a shop was gutted in the Plasmarl district of the town.

The brigade personnel that attended the fires were: Captain Colquhoun, Deputy Head Constable Gill, Inspectors Edwards and Nicholas, Sergeants Price, Hill, Jones and Lloyd, Constables Tomlinson, Flavin, J. Bounds, H. Davies, Thorne, Evans, W. Jones, J. Davies, E. Mills, Evans, Kennedy, G. Francis, Edgington, W. Francis, J. Jones, D. Davies, Hayes, Gregory, Thomas, Bevan, Gubb, and Benbow.

Deputy Head Constable Gill and Inspector Edwards, who had been in the force 35 years and 23 years respectively, agreed that the fire at the South Dock had been the biggest in their recollection. They added that the steamer '...had proved invaluable, pumping direct from the dock, provided a force so great, it required two men to direct the hose.' The fire at the South Dock included several premises in the vicinity, and was one of Swansea's worst, it was listed along with:

> Fatal fire in Temple Street, May 1866
> Fatal fire in Oxford Street/Beach Street, January 1883
> Destruction of the Fever Hospital, November 1883
> Strand Joinery Works, June 1890
> Stones Sawmills at the South Dock, August 1905
> Parry & Rocke's in the Strand, May 1906

Captain Colquhoun, at his monthly meeting with the Watch Committee, informed them that there had been 23 fires during the past month, some of a serious nature. The councillors applauded the fire brigade for their exertions at the recent fires, and also suggested that an extra engine should be purchased. Captain Colquhoun added:

...that if it had not been for the steamer, it would have been impossible to have prevented the spread of the fire, with regard to a further engine, if the Council obtained a motor fire engine, as he had suggested some time ago, it could also be used outside the Borough, thus overcoming that difficulty...

Swansea's Central Police Fire Brigade Station in Pleasant Street, although only opened in 1905, had been the centre of constant discussion about aspects of its accommodation. The original plans were altered, thereby reducing the finished station's dimensions, which resulted in a lack of accommodation for personnel and reduced the number of stables. As a result, in October 1909, the council acquired the old Ragged School. The acquisition and subsequent demolishing of the school would afford the necessary space for proposed enlargements to the central police fire brigade station.

In November 1909, the local press reported that the new Police Medal had been bestowed on Captain Colquhoun, along with other members of the police in the United Kingdom. Captain Colquhoun was described as a remarkable man, 'upright as a dart and as keen as the proverbial whistle, he carries his three score and ten years and more, with remarkable ease.' The following year, in June, the captain was officially presented with his medal by the new king, George V at a ceremony in London. The medal was struck by the command of the late king, Edward VII, and was intended for award to members of the police of the empire for conspicuous bravery. The medal was made of silver and its official inscription read: 'Captain Colquhoun, Chief Constable of Swansea Police – Awarded for long service, distinguished by exceptional ability and merit and marked by success in organising his Force.'

In August 1910, the village of Sketty, due to the Swansea council's proposed decision to charge outlying districts for the attendance of the borough brigade at outbreaks of fire, called a meeting at the Sketty Church minor hall to discuss the organisation of a fire brigade for the parish. The meeting, which was attended by several members of the parish, agreed that the following personnel would act as a volunteer fire brigade for the parish: Messrs R.F. Browne (Captain), Mr W. Davies (Vice Captain), Tom Morris (Secretary), S. Jenkins, J. Williams, W. Harris, J. Isaac, A. Green, Leslie Mears, Gwyn Davies, J. Llewellyn, Harry Edwards, James Benallack, W. Brown, H. Greber, H. Symonds, Fred Williams, E.J. Williams, C. Moss and S. Davies.

The Parish Council of Cockett had had fire-fighting apparatus for some time, but unfortunately they had fallen into disrepair. In September 1911, the volunteer firemen of that district protested about the fact that, following a call to a fire at neighbouring Sketty, they were unable to retrieve the hand cart from the fire station (shed) as it was locked up. The holder of the keys was ill in bed, and the members of the fire brigade had to walk two miles carrying the standpipes and hose. This, Captain Davies of the newly-formed Sketty fire brigade remarked, was totally unsatisfactory. He proposed that the captains of the respective brigades each be issued with a set of keys.

The need for the Swansea fire brigade to attend fires in the suburbs and outlying districts was evident. On a request from the Morriston police on 15 October 1911, they assisted at a fire in Woodfield Street, which resulted in the destruction of three shops. The local force had experienced difficulties with the over-enthusiastic crowds of people present. In their eagerness to assist, they damaged the standpipes and hose, and there were delays in obtaining water. It was not until the arrival of the Swansea brigade and extra constables that order prevailed. It was even reported that during the

confusion certain members of the crowd resorted to looting.

Also in October, the Swansea brigade attended a serious fire that had broken out in Old Road, Skewen, approximately six miles from Swansea. The fire, which broke out on Tuesday afternoon, 24 October 1911, started in the house of a local ice cream seller by the name of Ambrususisi, and within 10 minutes had become an inferno. The blaze quickly spread to adjoining premises, and consequently to the whole block, which consisted of four houses. There had been a delay in the Neath brigade's arrival, and as Skewen only had limited resources for coping with outbreaks of fire, the Briton Ferry brigade was also summoned. With a poor water supply, the Swansea and Briton Ferry engines (both steamers) resorted to obtaining water from a nearby brook. The members of the three brigades then set to work with a will, unfortunately not before the roofs of the three shops had fallen in. The resulting damage was estimated at around £1,500.

In February 1912, Gowerton, an outlying district some seven miles from Swansea, was the scene of a fire. A chapel in the village was ablaze, and the only

The Swansea fire brigade posing with the Shand Mason steam fire engine in 1906. The three officers in front are Inspector J.G. Edwards, Sergeant Davies and Deputy Chief Constable Gill. At the horse's head is Fireman John Davies. Standing on the fire engine are (from left to right) G. Edgington, P. Shear, E. Porter, J. Bounds, W. Good, and Tomlinson. High on the ladder are W. Bounds, Kennedy, E. Evans and Thorne. (Swansea fire brigade)

extinguishing agent available was a patent 'Fire Queen' extinguisher with a 50-gallon capacity. It was described as 'utterly useless, being little better than a squirt, on such a body of fire.'

Due to the severity of the blaze, the Swansea brigade was telephoned for, but they were unable to attend because they could not obtain 'shod' horses from the local stables. This once more raised the question of the brigade's attendance at outlying districts, to which Captain Colquhoun replied that 'if the outside Councils were to join Swansea in the expense of a motor fire engine, the whole question of Swansea's attendance to fires outside the Borough, would be a thing of the past.'

The re-organisation of the borough police force and fire brigade was still ongoing, and in May 1912 Mr Ernest Morgan, architect, submitted plans for the proposed extension of the central police fire brigade station. The plans incorporated a triangular piece of land abutting the Alexandra Road library on Orchard Street, and adjoining the present Pleasant Street station. If the scheme was adopted, the building would incorporate a police court, juvenile court, retiring rooms, police quarters, additional cells, and, on the Alexandra Road side, accommodation for the fire brigade and ambulance appliances. The estimated cost was £13,455.

Chapter Six

Forced to Change

The year 1912 saw the start of several changes to Swansea's police and fire brigade. In some ways it was the end of an era, as some of the best-known stalwarts resigned, some to be replaced by equally well-known names from within the borough force.

In May 1912, Inspector Edwards, referred to as the 'captain' of the fire brigade, resigned after 26 years. Inspector Edwards had spent the early part of his life at sea, and was twice shipwrecked, once on the coast of South Africa while on the SS *Clyde*, which at the time was conveying the famous '24th' to the Zulu War.

After his time in the navy, he joined the London fire brigade, which at the time was under the command of the famous Captain Eyre Massey Shaw. All of the 'captain's' men at that time were ex-seamen, and he believed them to have 'quickness of eye and foot.' It was while Captain Colquhoun was attending London in 1886, to observe the Metropolitan brigade's drills, that he observed Fireman Edwards and thought him a useful firemen. Later that day Captain Colquhoun struck up a conversation with Edwards, and eventually induced him to come to Swansea. This clarifies why Captain Colquhoun was so keen to make Edwards sergeant in charge of the fire brigade, a promotion which had, in June 1893,

caused controversy in the Watch Committee. Inspector Edwards attended no fewer than 2,600 fires in Swansea, and in all that time, only one person was burned to death, Mr Charles White, a blind man who lived at 104 Carmarthen Road in February 1904. When asked about the biggest fires he had attended Inspector Edwards replied that the worst were Parry & Rocke's in the Strand in 1905, and Glassbrook's Timber Yard in May 1909. It was with deep regret that the Swansea fire brigade accepted the resignation of Inspector Edwards. Under the Police Act 1890, he retired with a superannuation allowance of £1 19s 1d per week, which included his police and fire brigade service.

In September, following police promotions, the newly-promoted Inspector J. Bounds succeeded Inspector Edwards as 'captain' of the fire brigade. Inspector Bounds had joined the force on 3 September 1891, and, strange to say, was notified of his promotion on 3 September 1912. He also had a brother in the fire brigade, PC W. Bounds.

At a specially convened meeting on 8 November 1912, the Town Clerk, Mr Lang Coath, read a letter of resignation from the head constable, Captain Colquhoun. The captain had come to Swansea in 1877, when the town was half the size it was in 1912.

The police force had then comprised 52 men, but now the force numbered 152. Captain Colquhoun, at the age of 75, was still erect, alert and soldierly in his demeanour.

Captain Colquhoun had taken the Swansea fire brigade from being an average brigade in the 1800s, through to one that was respected and well thought. Its good conduct, experience and courage were well documented. At a farewell ceremony at the Guildhall, it was revealed that Captain Colquhoun, since taking over as Swansea's head constable, had trebled the number of officers in the force, improved pay and conditions and equipment, and raised Swansea to a force that was second to none in the United Kingdom.

The post of head constable was advertised in January 1913, and provoked responses from all over the United Kingdom. The deputy head constable, Mr Gill, had been declared too old, having turned 60 the previous July. The advert stated that the successful applicant would have to reside within the borough and must not be older than 45. The salary would be £550 per year. There were 35 applicants, and the Watch Committee had to reduce this to a shortlist of six. The final applicants were:

Colonel Carden, age 42, from Wiltshire
Lieutenant Evans, age 40, from Brynmill, Swansea
Captain Northern, age 39, from Essex
Captain Temple-Stone, age 38, from London
Inspector (Acting Superintendent) Alfred Thomas, age 38, from Nottingham
Captain Wakefield, age 37, from Nottingham

From the shortlist of six, the Watch Committee settled on two, one of whom would be the eventual head constable of Swansea. These final two were Mr Alfred Thomas, acting superintendent of the Nottinghamshire police force, who was also a native to Swansea. The other was Captain Wakefield, an adjutant to the Sherwood Foresters.

The decision to select Mr Alfred Thomas as Swansea's head constable was taken on the grounds of his experience in police work. However, it was felt by some of the other candidates that his appointment had more to do with the fact that he was a Swansea man.

Swansea's new chief of police, Captain Alf Thomas, was aged 38. He had served in the 3rd Glamorgan Volunteer Reserve, which eventually became the 6th Welsh, before joining the Nottinghamshire police force in 1904. He was promoted to sergeant in the chief constable's office under Mr Clay, who himself was an ex-Swansea man.

In the April a report was published which informed the council that Captain Thomas was unable to take up his post as chief constable. He had been hospitalised in Nottingham after a relapse following a bout of influenza, which had resulted in pneumonia. Captain Colquhoun was asked to remain in charge of the borough force. Although it appears that Captain Colquhoun did continue in his post for a short time, the length of Captain Thomas's illness meant that eventually the post of chief constable was taken over by Deputy Chief Constable Gill.

During this period of uncertainty, the Watch Committee announced further police and fire brigade promotions. As before, these engendered general dissatisfaction in the force, as some members felt that length of service had been overlooked. The promotions saw PC W. Bounds, brother of Inspector J. Bounds, become a sergeant, making him second in charge of the fire brigade.

The brigade, under the newly-promoted Sergeant Bounds, responded in June 1913 to an alarm of fire at the Swansea Vale Spelter Works, Llansamlet. The fire broke out a little after 7pm on Tuesday evening, resulting in an estimated £3,000-worth of damage. Three hundred men were rendered unemployed. So intense was the fire, that by the time the brigade arrived, their main course of action was to confine the flames to the six drying rooms, to prevent them from spreading to the adjoining buildings. The brigade, unfortunately, had been delayed in arriving because they were unable to obtain two horses from Bullin's stables. The steamer, due to its weight and the distance to travel, required four horses. Once the extra horses had been procured, the brigade was reported to have made splendid time in arriving at the scene. The brigade's difficulties with the engine did not end there. When the fire was eventually extinguished, the steamer, which had been positioned alongside the canal, had become stuck in the mud, and could only be extricated with great difficulty.

This was not the first time that the brigade had experienced difficulty in obtaining horses. However, on this occasion questions were raised at committee level and in the local press, about the need for Swansea to acquire a motor fire engine. The committee's response was to say that if a motor fire engine was required for a prompt and efficient service to outlying districts, then those districts should pay toward its cost.

This was a reasonable proposal if the public bodies acting on behalf of ratepayers in outlying areas were prepared to contribute to the costs incurred by the borough. The brigade had, after all, been established and equipped and maintained by the Swansea people, to deal with fires within the borough.

While the question of attending fires outside the borough was being discussed, the Mumbles district of West Cross was the scene of another fire on the site of the former Currant Tree Inn. Although the fire was serious, it was subdued by neighbours using a water supply from Mr Blackmaster's nurseries opposite. They used buckets, garden syringes, and a garden hose to fight the flames. The Mumbles police, although praised for their quick response, could only assist those already at the scene, as they had no additional firefighting equipment.

This fire provoked discussion among members of the Oystermouth District Council, which resulted in a report being submitted from the district surveyor and Sergeant Davies of the Mumbles police. The report concluded that if a fire brigade were formed, a manual engine, hose and fire escape would be required, the cost of which would be £432 11s 2d. A house to store the equipment would cost a further £400, and in addition to this, there would be the hire of horses.

The Mumbles council decided that the insurance companies should be contacted and asked to subscribe to the scheme. This resulted in a committee being formed, with the aim of obtaining the insurance companies' views on the matter.

In November 1913, Acting Chief Constable Gill tendered his resignation. He had served in the force for 39 years and had been promoted to Deputy Chief Constable in 1908. His resignation was to take effect from 2 January 1914, and caused further concern within the council about Captain Thomas's prolong-ed illness. Fortunately, Captain Thomas was deemed fit for duty after a medical examination, and was eventually able to take up his post as chief constable.

Another matter of concern was Swansea's water supply. The borough engineer, Mr Wyrill, was interviewed on the subject in January 1914. He reported that the Cray Reservoir scheme was in progress, along with the replacement of the water mains. Some of these mains were now posing health problems, as well as causing delays at outbreaks of fire. Some were so bad that either their internal diameters were greatly reduced, some by as much as nearly 60 per cent, or they were rusted so badly they could not withstand the pressure of the water in them. As a result of this, some of the new mains being installed from the reservoirs, those of 19 and 24 inches diameter, were made of concrete. This proved more satisfactory. Swansea was a pioneer in the use of concrete pipes as water mains.

At the beginning of 1914, it was proposed that Swansea, as a large and expanding town, should seriously consider the purchase of a motor fire engine. Morriston was also demanding better fire protection, as with their limited equipment and apparatus, they were reliant on the attendance of the Swansea brigade. This added weight to the arguments for purchasing a motor fire engine. The chief constable reported that Swansea had only one fire engine, which pumped 350 gallons per minute, and there was an urgent need for another appliance.

A serious fire occurred at the Mumbles on 1 March 1914, which involved three properties, all of which were seriously damaged, incurring costs estimated at several thousand pounds. The fire began on the premises of Mr W.H. Jones, a grocer and provisions merchant in Castleton. It was discovered by Edward Willing of 14 Chapel Street, Mumbles, as he was passing at about 4.10am. It was during a severe thunder storm, and it was thought that the fire started as a result of a telephone cable being struck by lightning, although this was disputed. When Willing first noticed the flames and volumes of smoke in the shop, he alerted the residents before informing the local police. Inspector Davies and six constables arrived on the scene, but having no firefighting equipment, they could do nothing, and soon the scene was a mass of flames. Seeing the seriousness of the fire, at 4.30am Inspector Davies telephoned the Swansea fire brigade, who were at the scene with the engine at 5.15am, under the command of Inspector Bounds and his crew, which consisted of Constables Evans, Davies, Bevan, O'Brian, and Blackmore. The heat was so terrific that the glass windows of houses opposite cracked. A large portion of the wall was displaced, and fell with a crash to the ground, narrowly missing Inspector Davies and one of the Swansea firemen. The Swansea brigade eventually extinguished the fire, and returned to the station at 7.30am. So intense had the fire been, that a local firm

was employed to demolish the building, since the walls were in a precarious condition.

Some local councillors who visited the scene the following morning, were given a difficult time by the locals. The fire had once more emphasised the need for adequate fire appliances for the village. The equipment that had been provided by the district council was deemed to be useless, and until the arrival of the Swansea brigade, the police and neighbours were ineffectual. Due to the seriousness of the situation, the Oystermouth District Council accepted tenders for the erection of a fire station for the Oystermouth and Mumbles areas. One was from

The scene following the fire at W.H. Jones, grocers, in Castleton, Mumbles in March 1914. The building (obviously no longer a grocers) is also pictured after it was rebuilt. (Mrs Wendy Cope)

Messrs Beynon Bros for £62 7s 6d, while the other was from Messrs J.G. Morris for £54 8s. The lower tender was then accepted. The site for the proposed station, which was nothing more than a shed, was on land adjacent to the council chambers, the library in Park Street, which fronted near The Dunns, at the rear of the Methodist church. The council also agreed to purchase hose and equipment from Shand Mason at a cost of £107 12s 9d, and an escape ladder for £83.

Swansea's borough clerk, Mr Roderick, informed the Watch Committee that 14 replies had been received from outside district councils regarding contributions to the cost of a motor fire engine. Some were favourable, others were not.

In May 1914, representatives of the district authorities attended a meeting of the Swansea Watch Committee, to discuss the question of contributions to a motor fire engine. The borough treasurer, Mr Ashmole, informed the meeting that he envisaged three ways in which the districts could pay contributions to the Swansea council.

1. The district council could levy a three-quarters of a penny rate.
2. There could be a scale of charges, and the Corporation would undertake to administrate the scheme and issue bills for certain charges to the districts.
3. The district councils could contribute a lump sum to the fund for the engine.

A further proposal was put forward suggesting a mileage and time rate. Before any decision was made, it was proposed that an estimate for the cost of a motor fire engine, and its running and upkeep, be obtained.

Following the meeting, an editorial appeared in the press, stating that 'unless the Authorities of the outside areas are prepared to pay what is tantamount to an insurance premium against fire, they and their constituents must not be surprised if the services of the Swansea Fire Brigade are reserved strictly for those contributing to its equipment and upkeep.' In

the event that the district councils did not contribute, they should be compelled to adopt one of the three courses named, or provide and organise their own means for fighting fire, co-operate in a financial sense with Swansea, or accept the risk of having fires without the means of combating them. A motor fire engine, it was thought would be most of use outside the borough. If it were to be employed in that capacity, it should, in part at least, be paid for by those communities which chiefly stood to benefit from it.

The Bath & West Show was held at Victoria Park in May, the fire cover for which was provided by Messrs Merryweather's of Greenwich, London. As Swansea was considering the purchase of a motor fire engine, Merryweather's fire brigade exhibited and displayed their new model motor fire engine to Captain Thomas and the Swansea Watch Committee. It was first displayed outside the Ben Evans Store in Castle Street, where it threw a jet of water high over the top of the building. It was then taken to Ferryside, near the town's Guildhall, where it pumped water from the South Dock basin, providing four jets of great force. Both displays created a great deal of interest, especially from the customary large crowds which attended Swansea's fires and displays.

At their next meeting, on 16 June 1914, Swansea's Watch Committee reported that a deputation had been sent to London to witness certain tests, which were considered to be totally satisfactory. As a result, a decision was taken to purchase a 'Dennis turbine fire engine,' from Dennis Bros of Guildford, at a cost of £1,135. It was of the latest type, which was currently being used in most towns and cities, and would be fully equipped, complete with a detachable 55ft escape ladder. Although the initial order for the engine was placed in 1914, Swansea did not take delivery until March 1915.

Swansea's new central police fire brigade station, referred to as a 'commodious new building,' was opened by the then mayor, Alderman Dan Jones, on

Swansea fire brigade turning out from the Alexandra Road fire station with the steamer, on 29 April 1915. (Swansea Reference Library)

28 April 1915. It had been erected at an estimated cost of £23,000, and was built by the firm of Messrs Weavers & Co. of Swansea. The designer was Swansea architect, Mr Ernest Morgan, who had taken full advantage of an awkwardly-shaped site, which even incorporated the older police fire brigade station in Pleasant Street, which was extended, and brought into the general scheme. Within the station tower was a four-faced public clock, built by Mr Webber of Oxford Street, Swansea, and donated by Alderman Evan Evans at a cost of £400.

The outbreak of World War One coincided with the opening of the new station and the purchase of the motor engine, and resulted in a directive being sent from the Home Office to the Chief Constable's Association. It stated that:

> In the Secretary of State's opinion, it is desirable that the recruitment for the Police, of men of military age who might enlist, should be suspended or reduced to the narrowest possible limits for the period of the war. If the vacancies in any Force can be temporarily made good by the temporary appointment of constables, or by the employment as Special Constables or pensioners and others who are prevented from enlisting by age or any other good reason, this should be done in preference to filling vacancies in the regular Force by the recruitment of men who might otherwise join H.M. Forces, and so long as arrangements are made for the efficient performance of necessary police duties, no Force will be reported by the Government Inspector as inefficient, merely because the regular Police is below strength.

The Swansea Police, like other police during World War One, suffered from men leaving the ranks to enlist. This, as the previous directive had stated, meant that the force was augmented by special constables, whose services were also used in the fire brigade.

The War Office issued a directive to authorities which employed a fire brigade in 1915, urging them to endeavour to recruit men who were not eligible for the army as substitute firemen. They should encourage active co-operation with their local Volunteer Training Corps, or similar organisations, for part-time assistance, as had so successfully been arranged in London. Several private fire brigades connected with establishments engaged in government work were understaffed due to enlistment, and some of them employed women to make up the shortfall. Today we consider the concept of women firefighters a modern one, but, although there was a chauvinistic attitude towards them, Burton in Staffordshire employed female firefighters as early as 1911.

The newly formed Sketty parish brigade also encountered problems due to enlistment. The parish council was informed that, due to members of the brigade having joined up, the appliances were not being kept as they should. It was suggested that the

county police be contacted and asked to take over the responsibility for acting as a fire brigade for the district. Whether the county police did act as a fire brigade is unclear, as there are no further reports of the Sketty parish council fire brigade. The district of Sketty eventually became part of Swansea under the borough extension scheme, and fire cover for the district was then provided by the borough brigade.

In accordance with the promise given by the Oystermouth District Council, the Mumbles district had its own fire brigade. The local Volunteer Artillery Detachment (VAD), commanded by Commandant C. Russell Pennock, was instructed in the use of the fire equipment supplied by the council, by PC Thorne of the Swansea fire brigade.

The effectiveness of Swansea's motor fire engine was demonstrated in July 1916, when the brigade received a report of a fire at the Raven Tin Plate Works, Glanamman. They responded to the call at 7.30am, and reportedly arrived at 8.10am, having covered a distance of approximately 20 miles. Their promptness on this occasion was a stark contrast to the fire they attended with the horse steamer in November 1908.

The borough brigade attended two serious outbreaks of fire in December 1917. The first was at Drymma Hall, a large mansion-type building that had been converted into a mental hospital, approximately seven miles from Swansea, and outside the borough limits. Again the brigade were reported to have arrived at the scene remarkably promptly. The fire occurred at just after 3am, and the firefighters remained at the scene until noon. The hall was virtually destroyed and sustained damage costed at £15,000.

The second fire occurred at the Pacific Patent Fuel Works, near the entrance of the Prince of Wales dock, on 30 December 1917. The fire was discovered by the night watchman a little after 5am, when the flames had already burst through the roof. The brigade, under the command of Inspector Edgar Evans, was

Swansea's first motorised fire engine, a 1915 Dennis pump escape. (Surrey County Council)

soon in attendance, and with little or no hope of saving the main building, they concentrated their efforts on confining the blaze and preventing it from spreading to the adjoining buildings. The brigade were assisted by the Harbour Trust tug boat, *Trusty*, which pumped large volumes of water on to the flames. It was not until 1pm that the fire was finally subdued. The damage was estimated at £10,000–£15,000, and the blaze left 150 men unemployed.

The chief constable, Captain Thomas, in his monthly report in February 1919, informed the Watch Committee that during World War One, 77 members of the borough force had enlisted in His Majesty's Forces, nine of whom were killed. As a consequence of the war, the force had recruited 238 volunteers, or 'specials', of whom some did invaluable police work, while the others assisted with ambulance and fire brigade duties. They were rewarded for their devotion to duty. The *London Gazette* reported that all specials that had completed not less than three years service would be issued with a Special Constabulary Medal by the government, and that names should be forwarded to the Home Secretary by all chief constables.

Swansea was again troubled by a fire with tragic consequences on 19 November 1919. PC 103 May, who was on his beat in the Argyle Street area of the town, heard shouts of 'Fire!' and saw volumes of smoke issuing from 100 Oxford Street, a grocer's shop kept by Mr Rosser and his wife. On arrival at the scene, he heard piercing cries from an upstairs room. With the shop already a mass of flames, the young constable went round to the rear via the next door property, where he obtained a ladder. Then, with the assistance of a neighbour, he placed the ladder to the upstairs window, where Mrs Rosser was precariously standing. While he was ascending the ladder, the unfortunate Mrs Rosser fell or jumped, and landed heavily on the flag-stoned yard, breaking her leg. The constable was told that Mrs Elizabeth Phillips, aged

70 and bedridden, was still inside the house. PC May entered the bedroom to search for her, which was hazardous, as the fire had taken such a hold that the floor was beginning to give way. PC May continued with his quest and eventually came across the body of the unfortunate lady, which was charred beyond recognition.

While the young constable had been carrying out his rescue, the fire brigade had been summoned by the tramcar driver, Mr Clifford, who had initially come across the fire on his way to work. Although prompt in their attendance, the brigade experienced difficulty in obtaining water because of a lack of pressure. Once water was available, however, the fire was quickly subdued. No.100 Oxford Street was reduced to a smouldering ruin, and the adjoining properties were badly damaged.

During his heroic attempts to rescue the old lady, PC May suffered severe lacerations to his hands and arms, from broken glass, and he needed hospital treatment. On Monday 24 November, Mrs Rosser, who had suffered a broken thigh when she fell from the window, died of her injuries in Swansea Hospital. For his bravery, PC 103 C.G. May was awarded a certificate.

At the monthly Watch Committee meeting on 25 November 1919, the chief constable reported that the strength of the brigade was 21 members, and its appliances and equipment included two horses, one motor fire engine, one tender, 11 hand escapes, 15 hand hose carts, and 5,100 yards of hose. The appliances he considered to be in good order, but in order to keep the brigade in a state of efficiency, a further motor fire engine was required.

The committee discussed the chief constable's proposal with the borough treasurer, which resulted in an order for a motor fire engine being placed with Dennis Bros. of Guildford, at an estimated cost of £1,440. The appliance would be fitted with a four-cylinder White & Poppe 45hp engine, and a Gwynne turbine pump capable of pumping 350 gallons per

The Cameron Hotel, High Street, Swansea, the scene of a serious fire in April 1920. (Swansea Reference Library)

minute. This was delivered on Friday 8 October 1920, and the following morning it was driven to the South Dock, where, under the watchful eyes of the public, who had thronged to the area in curiosity, the pump was put through its paces.

Shortly after 12.20pm on 28 April 1920, a major fire occurred at one of Swansea's most prestigious hotels, the Hotel Cameron in the High Street (now the site of the Argos store). The brigade responded with their usual promptness, but were hampered by the crowds of people who had rushed to the area when they saw the flames and smoke. Inspector Edgar Evans and his men soon had the appliances working, supplied with hydrants from the Strand and the High Street. At 1pm the store rooms, where the fire had originated, were described as 'a burning furnace', and the roof of the hotel at the rear had fallen in, which threatened the upper bedrooms. This was where the brigade directed their attention, as anxiety was felt by the Unitarian Church Authorities, whose chapel was only a short distance from the store room. As a precaution a hose was run out through the chapel, but fortunately it was not required.

The seriousness of the outbreak could be appreciated by a glance at the rear of the hotel, which was nothing more than a skeleton of charred timber roof joists. By 1.30pm the blaze had been all but mastered, but the damage was estimated at around £45,000 for the hotel's structure and contents. Thankfully the damage was mainly confined to the rear portion of the hotel, and the front portion remained virtually intact, allowing some business to be carried on.

Some two months after the Cameron Hotel fire, the Swansea fire brigade was confronted with another fire, this time at Lewis' timber yard, on the river side of the Prince of Wales dock, on Monday 7 June. The alarm was received at the fire station shortly after 10pm, and Inspector Evans and his men responded with their customary smartness. On their arrival they found the works and its timber stocks already a mass of roaring flame and smoke, ascending many hundreds of feet into the night sky. The brigade, due to the proximity of the River Tawe, had an unlimited supply of water. The motor fire engine, with its powerful pump, was able to supply four jets, which were directed on to the burning mass almost immediately. The timber yard was already doomed, so the brigade's exertions were concentrated on saving the adjoining buildings, the Cape Copper Company and a warehouse owned by the Harbour Trust Authorities. Unfortunately, their efforts were not rewarded, as both buildings were gutted. Throughout the fire, the brigade was assisted by numerous volunteers: former soldiers, seamen and members of the workforce, all of whom rendered invaluable assistance in removing the timber, most of which was thrown into the river.

The glare from the blaze had illuminated the whole of the docks area, and the customary hoards of sightseers made their way to the scene to investigate. What they saw was described as 'a rich pink glow that hung above the town's docks,' and even the River Tawe was described as 'a pool of rippled gold in the reflection of the fire, with the occasional dark raft of timber floating within, some of the baulks still glowing red, or even alight.'

The brigade worked strenuously throughout the night, then shortly after 10am on Tuesday morning, 12 hours after the alarm was raised, the blaze was controlled and reduced to smoke arising from smouldering planks, which were being separated from the untouched timber. The inspector and his men returned to their station just after noon.

The *South Wales Daily Post* reported on 17 May 1921 that Captain Alfred Thomas, Swansea's chief constable, had died. He had passed away in the early hours of the morning, following prolonged ill health, despite a six-month leave of absence to recuperate in Switzerland. Captain Thomas, following his appointment as Swansea's chief constable in February 1913, had been unable to take up his post due to ill health, which at the time had led to disagreements within the Watch Committee.

The captain's death provoked disagreement within the committee, when a decision was taken to promote the deputy chief constable, Mr R.D. Roberts, to the post. As he was already aged 58, a section of the committee believed that the town would benefit from a younger man, and that the post

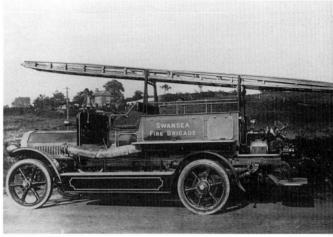

Swansea fire brigade's Dennis fire engine, September 1920. (Surrey County Council)

should be advertised. However, it was decided by majority vote that Mr Roberts should be Captain Thomas's successor, subject to Home Office approval.

The new chief constable had been born in Ffestiniog in North Wales, and had been a member of the borough force for 32 years. During this time he had worked his way through the ranks, becoming a superintendent in 1914, and then deputy chief constable. Interestingly, in 1913 he had been debarred from applying for the post chief constable, as at 50 years of age he was considered too old. The age limit, fixed at that time by the Watch Committee, was 40.

Swansea's main thoroughfare, Gower Street (the present Kingsway), was the scene of an alarming fire that engulfed a whole block of buildings on 29 June 1921. The brigade was called shortly before midnight. When they arrived the premises of Mr Barron Pascoe, Estate Agent, Hutchinson's drapers, Palmer's carriage and motor works, and Price Rees and Co., house decorators, were all already well alight, and flames were shooting into the night sky, probably fuelled by the flammable contents of the shops. The fire brigade soon had jets playing on the fire, and some were directed on to the flames from adjoining rooftops. The desired effect was achieved, and they were able to prevent the flames from spreading to the nearby Co-operative Stores. However, the premises of Price Rees, Palmer and Hutchinson's were completely destroyed by the time the blaze was subdued at 3am the following morning.

The brigade had been extremely busy of late, not only having to attend to fires within the confines of the town and borough, but also responding to fires at Mumbles and Clydach. The outbreak at Clydach occurred at around 10.30pm on 10 November, at the Globe Cinema, and its spectacular nature attracted a vast crowd of spectators. The heat was so intense that it was feared that the houses and shops on the opposite side of the street might catch fire too. The Swansea brigade, under the command of Inspector Evans, were on the scene, with jets playing on the premises adjoining the cinema. These included an ironmongers shop and a warehouse, both of which contained oil and paint. Had it not been for the timely intervention of the Swansea brigade, the outbreak might have had far more serious results.

With the opening of an oil refinery at Llandarcy, near Skewen, in 1921, Swansea's Queen's Dock became a thriving oil port. Tankers discharging their cargoes posed further problems for Swansea's firefighters in subsequent years. On the evening of 17 November 1921, what was probably the Swansea brigade's first fire aboard an oil tanker occurred when a fire broke out on the *British Tommy*. On this occasion, thankfully, the blaze was contained, and extinguished within a few hours.

The Baldwin's Hermatite Works in Landore, which had produced shells for the war effort, was the scene of a serious blaze at around 2.30pm on 1 May 1922. The Swansea brigade fought the blaze for over six hours. The brigade had an ample supply of water, as with their now two-year-old Dennis they were able to set into the nearby River Tawe. Unfortunately, due to the design of the building, they were limited by a lack of openings to direct their jets through, and were unable to enter through the normal doorways because of the intense heat. They had no alternative other than to continue pouring the water on to the blaze via the high windows. For over an hour this had little or no effect, but the brigade continued to battle. They were eventually rewarded some hours later, when the fire began to show signs of abating.

At around 1.10pm on Wednesday 8 October 1924, Goat Street, one of Swansea's main streets, was rocked by a gas explosion on the premises of Messrs T.W. James, Solicitors, which was situated next to and adjoined the Jewish synagogue. Apparently, just before the explosion, a man who had been delivering coal to the cellar beneath T.W. James's offices had been overcome by fumes. This was thought to have been caused by a gas leak, and he had been taken to hospital and the gas company informed.

The scene in the street following the explosion was indescribable. The other men that had been unloading the coal were lying in the roadway smothered in blood, the pavement and the road were strewn with debris and office furniture, which had been blown through the windows, littered the street. Flames were emanating from the building. The fire brigade, under the command of Inspector Evans, had to place a ladder across where the floor had once been in order to gain entry to the building. In this way they were able to help the men and women who had been working in the office out of the building. Even with the building empty, the brigade were unable to extinguish the fire, which by this time was burning furiously, until gas works employees disconnected the supply. Once this was done the blaze was extinguished at around 3pm.

A young errand boy named Brinley Rees, of King Street, who had been passing when the explosion took place, was caught in the initial blast and killed instantly. Over 20 people had been injured, eight seriously. The caretaker, Mrs Elizabeth Davies, who had been trapped in the cellar following the blast and had been rescued by a passer-by, died of her injuries five weeks later, bringing the death toll to two.

A local newspaper reported on 25 October 1924 that the death had occurred of one of Swansea's fire heroes, Thomas 'Tommy' Tucker. He had been decorated for rescues at fires at Tontine Street, in 1893, for which he received the Quiver Medal, and again in the High Street in 1902, for his remarkable rescue of six people, for which he received the Royal Humane Society for the Protection of Life from Fire medal. Thomas Tucker had died at his home in George Street, Swansea, aged 73. He had retired from the Swansea Brigade in 1914, after completing 25 years service.

Serious fires in Swansea continued to occur, and in February 1925 a fire that threatened three business premises broke out in the High Street, in the chemist shop of Messrs Harris and Morris. There was also a large and destructive fire at the Cwmfelin Tin Plate Works, off Llangyfelach Road in Swansea. The fire, which had broken out in a store room, and spread quickly through the piles of wooden boxes used for despatch purposes, resulted in the collapse of the roof. Fireman Harris was slightly injured during the firefighting.

One of the most destructive fires that occurred in 1925 was on 22 September. Hundreds of people stood and watched a fire in a block of buildings in Northampton Lane, in the town centre. The buildings were partly occupied by Messrs Betts, mineral water manufacturers, and at one time it was believed that fire had broken out following an explosion of gas from some machinery. Although the fire in Betts's was brought under control relatively quickly, the same could not be said for Mr James's workshop, which adjoined the building. He was a cabinet manufacturer, and because of the large amount of timber and furniture stored in the workshop, the firemen experienced severe difficulties in subduing the blaze. The workshop was totally destroyed, leaving nothing more than the remains of charred rafters.

Then at the close of the year, on 28 December, a fire broke out at the Mackworth Hotel in the High Street. The fire had originated in a maid's room at the top of the hotel, and rapidly spread via a lift shaft down to the bakery on the ground floor at the rear. Although the fire brigade had been sent for, a constable on duty in the police station across the road in Orchard Street also saw the smoke and gave the alarm. The brigade, under the command of Inspector Evans, arrived, only to find that the back portion of the hotel in Orchard Street was well alight. There was grave concern for Llewellyn's warehouse, situated across the narrow Tower Lane. Apart from the warehouse, the store's garage was close by, within which there were some motor vehicles and a petrol supply. The brigade did have to quell a small fire that had broken out in the warehouse's millpuff store. With hydrants in use from Alexandra Road, Orchard Street and the High Street, the firemen had an ample supply of water, and were able to confine the fire to the rear portion of the hotel. However, during the fire, there was concern about the fact that the hotel's wall, abutting Tower Lane, was showing signs of bulging due to the strain from the heat.

The horrors of working in a smoke-filled environment, unless experienced, can only be imagined. At this time the Swansea brigade had no breathing apparatus, and their only protection against smoke, if it could be called that, was a wet handkerchief over the nose and mouth. At a fire in a piano shop in St Helen's Road on 16 March 1926, the brigade were confronted with belching white smoke issuing from the shop's doorways, windows and the cellar ventilators. A large quantity of wooden packing cases containing straw were involved in the fire, and this, together with the fact that the fire was in the shop's cellar, added to the difficulties. In order to reach the seat of the fire, the firemen had to resort to knocking a hole through the cellar wall from an adjoining cellar, then, with nothing more than a wet handkerchief placed over the mouth and nose, they had to fight the blaze. The fire, although com-

Weaver's Flour Mill, with its connecting bridge, which suffered a serious outbreak of fire on 24 June 1926. (Swansea Reference Library)

paratively small, was extremely difficult to subdue, and a fireman named Morris was overcome by the smoke. He was conveyed to his home to recuperate.

From the reports of the fire, it seemed that the fire had only been extinguished by removing the floorboards from the floor of the shop above and street-level gratings from the pavement. The firemen's hoses were then directed through these openings in order to flood the cellar.

The firemen again had to resort to the use of handkerchiefs as face masks in order to contend with smoke at a blaze at the Graigola Works at Swansea's Kings Dock.

Swansea's well-known dockland landmark, Weaver's Flour Mill, was the scene of a historic fire at just after midnight on 24 June 1926. Situated at the entrance of the North Dock, the main building was one side of the Harbour road, with its large grain silo opposite.

These two buildings were connected by means of a single-span bridge. Despite the lateness of the hour, the fire had attracted the customary crowds of spectators. When the brigade arrived they were confronted by a serious blaze. A copious supply of water was obtained from the nearby Beaufort Dock. The firemen were soon at work playing their jets on to the flames. The main building had been equipped with a sprinkler system, which informed everyone that it was operating by the clattering of its bell, this, along with the assistance of the mill's own fire brigade, had been instrumental in saving the main building from destruction.

The fire had spread to the overhead connecting bridge, igniting its wooden structure, which gave great concern to the firefighters. It was feared that if the bridge collapsed, it would bring with it the side of the building. In the hope of preventing this, the firemen directed their jets to cool the main supports and prevent them from buckling. The Cuba Hotel and several dwelling houses were close by, and the anxiety of the residents can only be imagined, as most of them were outside in the streets, many only in their night attire. Their fears were eventually allayed, as all the buildings, apart from the Cuba Hotel, which suffered some scorching, escaped unscathed. Also beneath Weaver's span bridge was the high level Great Western Railway line and live tram wires, all of which had caused concern during the outbreak. The works and borough brigades did all in their power to quell the flames, and a 'doughty band of volunteers' set about attempting to rescue seven of the company's lorries. Unfortunately, while in the process of pushing one to safety, the others, loaded and waiting to go out on deliveries, speedily caught fire.

Although the fire had showed signs of abating just after 2am, sparks continued to float into the night air from the still smouldering debris. Some of the firemen had continued to work throughout the night and into the following afternoon, some completing over 14 hours without relief.

Weaver's Flour Mill, while in a derelict condition, was the scene of a further fire on 23 October 1965. It then became unsafe, and was consequently demolished. Weaver's was on the site currently occupied by the Sainsbury's Store in Quay Parade. The main Weaver's building had a claim to having been the first concrete building of its type in the world.

On Friday 3 March 1927, the *South Wales Daily Post* reported the sudden death of the Swansea fire brigade's ex-inspector, John George Edwards. Since joining the brigade in 1883, he had become the driving force behind the Swansea fire brigade. Apart from taking an active part in its training and organisation, he was also well known for training personnel in Swansea's neighbouring brigades. He was a prominent figure in the fire brigade photographs of the time, often accompanied by his terrier dog Jack.

In August 1927, the Welsh Agricultural Show was held in Singleton Park. While attending the opening day, the then chief constable, Mr R.D. Roberts, collapsed. Although he received medical attention at the show and was taken to his home in Carnglas Road in Sketty, he died of a heart seizure at a little after 1am the following morning.

Captain Roberts had only held the position of chief constable since May 1921, and now, for the third time in 11 years, the Watch Committee had to appoint a successor. After advertising the post, Swansea received nearly 100 applications, from which a short list of eight was drawn up. After the interviewing procedures, Captain Roberts's successor was appointed. Swansea's new chief constable was Mr Thomas Rawson, ex-chief constable of Hereford.

The annual fire brigade conference was held in Portsmouth in June 1928, and was attended by the Swansea Watch Committee chairman, Sir Percy Molineux. He reported back to the committee about a new turntable ladder that had been demonstrated. It could be mounted on one of three chassis, was 85ft high and self-supporting, so it could be used as a water tower. With a sling attachment, it could also be used for effecting rescues. Whether the new chief constable had attended the conference was not reported. However, at the monthly meeting on Tuesday 26 June, the chief constable informed the meeting that the firefighting facilities in Swansea were, in his belief, 'quite inadequate to deal effectively with a major outbreak'. The last important fire appliances had been purchased by Swansea in 1915 and 1920, and since then there had been no addition.

Swansea fire brigade posing for a photograph with their fleet of appliances in Pleasant Street, Swansea, in 1930. The two main officers in front are Inspector Francis Winteringham and Chief Constable F.J. May. (Swansea fire brigade)

After a discussion the Watch Committee, on the recommendation of the chief constable, agreed to purchase a new tower escape (known today as a turntable ladder), at a cost of £3,200.

At the August meeting a list of turntable escapes, their manufacturers and costs was provided. Merryweather had written saying that they had an all-British appliance, but unfortunately it would not be available for another month. It cost £2,550. Then there was the Morris/Magirus at a cost of £2,610, which was also fitted with its own integral pump. The final appliance on the list was a Leyland/Metz, at a cost of £2,458, which was designed to tow a trailer turbine pump, manufactured by Dennis and costing a further £400, the total estimated cost being £2,858. The Leyland was recommended by the chief constable, and he added that with the initial cost of £3,200 being agreed to by the committee, the purchase of the Leyland would be at a saving of £342 on the original estimate. The committee agreed to the purchase of the Leyland turntable ladder and a Dennis trailer pump.

This was the start of the new chief constable's regime of updating the Swansea fire brigade and its equipment. There was even a quip in the local newspaper about the fire brigade's costs, which said 'Swansea is to spend £3,200 on a water tower to fight fires, all our fires should be held on rainy days.'

The following September, the brigade took delivery of the Dennis trailer pump, which was reputed to deliver 400 gallons per minute. It was put through its paces at a demonstration in Somerset Place, in front of a large crowd. First it was worked from the quay, then fed by a hydrant supply. This effectively demonstrated the ease with which the pump could be handled in narrow inaccessible locations, with only a few men.

At around noon on Thursday 7 September 1928, what was described as yet another serious and destructive fire that Swansea had encountered in recent years, occurred at Glassbrook's timber yard at the South Dock. The fire not only destroyed the timber yard, but also the offices of Messrs Fred W. Davies, builders merchants. The brigade's newly-acquired trailer pump showed its versatility. It was towed to the scene by the 'Black Maria' which also provided much-needed extra hose. During the fire PC Tom Davies had a narrow escape when a huge portion of the builder's corrugated iron wall fell in. By 3pm the building had been reduced to a smouldering mass of timber and ashes, but the firemen remained at the scene, damping down the remains until 9.30pm. Two men stayed all night. Throughout the blaze, which was the chief constable's first in charge, he had remained in attendance, accompanied by Superintendent Bowen and Sergeant Kennedy.

A loan for the purchase of the turntable ladder had been agreed to by the Ministry of Health. The chief constable further added that a hand-propelled escape ladder, purchased in 1906, had been sold to the Inverness Town Council for £35. Further equipment was soon forthcoming for the brigade's use. This consisted of a 'smoke helmet' to replace the ineffective wet handkerchiefs. The design was similar to a divers helmet, with a glass front. Air was pumped into it from a bellows by way of an attached pipe. This new piece of equipment was eventually put to good use, when on Thursday 12 September 1929, the fire brigade received a report of a fire on the premises of Messrs Godfrey & Company, St Helen's Road, Swansea. On their arrival they found that the building was smoke filled, but after donning the smoke helmets the firemen were able reach the seat of the fire. It was successfully extinguished with far more ease than on previous occasions.

September 1929 also saw the retirement of the brigade's 'chief', Inspector Edgar Evans. He had joined the force in 1902, then following his promotion to inspector in 1917, he took charge of the fire brigade. His post was temporarily filled by Sergeant Kennedy, who took the title of acting inspector with Constable Frederick Morris as his deputy. However, Sergeant Kennedy, at 49, was eligible to retire, and as a result of this the chief constable recommended that an expert in fire brigade procedures should be appointed. This, he believed, would be better achieved by advertising the post and employing from 'outside' – preferably a younger man who would be full of energy and hold a diploma from the Institute of Fire Engineers.

The chief constable, Thomas Rawson, succeeded in convincing the Watch Committee that the new fire brigade chief should be an experienced outsider. In October 1929 this resulted in the appointment of Sergeant Francis Winteringham, aged 32, who had joined the Leeds City Fire Brigade in 1925 as chief engineer. He was now promoted to inspector of the Swansea Brigade as successor to Edgar Evans.

With the police as well as the fire brigade undergoing a period of transformation, Chief Constable Rawson decided that it would be more economical and more efficient to replace some police stations with the new concept of 'police call boxes'. These would be installed in outlying districts as well as in strategic locations around the town, and would make it easier for the public to contact the police and thus the fire brigade.

The fire brigade was summoned to a serious fire at No.8 Wassail Square, Swansea from the St Mary's police box on Monday 17 March 1930. The call was received at 12.32am, and the brigade responded under the command of its new chief, Inspector Winteringham, accompanied by Sergeant Kennedy and nine firemen. They took to the scene the pump escape CY 3 and a tender (presumably the trailer pump).

The brigade promptly set to work, with jets from the main street. Inspector Winteringham was informed that there were still people inside the building, but owing to the shouting and crying of women he was unable to ascertain how many. After two unsuccessful attempts to get up the stairs, which

were impassable on account of flames, the inspector, leading by example, ascended a ladder and entered through the first floor window. He located Thomas Bullin, aged 14, in the front room near the door, and handed him through the window to another fireman on the ladder. The inspector continued his search, hampered by the burning stairs, and eventually entered a back bedroom, only to find it empty. At this point he was joined by PC 103 Price, and together they continued up the staircase to the second floor. They entered the front bedroom and Price located and rescued George Bradley, carrying him down the stairs and handing him out through the first floor window to a waiting fireman. In the meantime, Inspector Winteringham had found a third person, Mrs Mary Sydenham, in the back bedroom. Owing to the seriousness of her condition, he deemed it inadvisable to attempt to carry her down the still burning staircase. However, he was joined by Fireman 152 Morris, and the two wrapped her in a blanket and carried her down the stairs and out to the safety of nearby Sullivan's lodging house.

Elsie Sydenham, aged 20, had jumped from a first floor window before the fire brigade arrived and broken her wrist. She and all three people rescued by the fire brigade were taken to the Swansea General Hospital, where unfortunately Mrs Mary Sydenham died a few days later from the burns she received.

In the months that followed, the Swansea Watch Committee recommended that the three firemen that had shown considerable bravery at the Wassail Square fire should be recognised. This resulted in Inspector Francis Winteringham and Police Constables 103 David Price and 152 Frederick Hollister Morris being awarded the Humane Society for the Protection of Life from Fire Bronze Medal.

As a consequence of the selling off of some of the outlying police stations, which were replaced by call boxes, some districts lost their fire appliances. This was, however, considered acceptable, as the fire brigade was fully motorised and it was thought that

Police Fireman Alan 'Jinks' Jenkins (1925–1955). (Mrs Perman, daughter)

there would be little delay in responding to fires. These surplus fire appliances, like the stations, were sold off. One such sale saw a hand-operated fire escape purchased by the Cardigan borough for £20, and the Landore police station in Field Street became a public library.

In August 1930 the Swansea brigade took delivery of its new Leyland/ Metz 85ft turntable ladder, which was duly demonstrated to the onlooking Watch Committee at the rear of the Alexandra Road fire station. Further equipment was added by means of a 'Davy Escape'. This was a friction brake rescue device that enabled people to be lowered to the ground, either from the turntable ladder or a building. Also acquired was a foam generator for use on oil or petrol fires.

The Swansea brigade, in previous years, had been found lacking in appliances and equipment, compared to some of its neighbouring fire brigades. This situation changed with the appointment of Thomas Rawson as chief constable. He brought the Swansea Brigade up to date, and even surpassed some other brigades.

On Friday 5 September 1930, the Swansea brigade, under Sergeant Kennedy, travelled to the Mumbles, where the former fire station, opposite the Wesleyan Chapel in the Dunns, was well alight. There were no longer any fire appliances or equipment on the premises, and unfortunately there seems to be no record of whether the fire brigade in the Mumbles had been disbanded or not. The district may, by this time, have been reliant on the Swansea brigade. The former fire station, which had been used by the council as stables since the fire brigade had vacated it, was completely destroyed in the blaze.

Chief Constable Rawson, although he had only held his post for a little over three years, had had a huge impact. Under his leadership Swansea became one of the most progressive brigades in the country, and had the benefit of Rawson's innovative ideas on equipment and extra mechanised appliances. However, in January 1931 the chief constable announced his intention to accept the post of chief constable of Bradford. Once again, the Watch Committee had the unenviable task of appointing a successor.

The post was advertised, and once again a large number of applicants applied. Eventually a short list was drawn up, mostly of candidates from English constabularies. Finally, on 3 March, Chief

Superintendent F.J. May of the Sheffield force was appointed as successor to Thomas Rawson. Frank Joseph May had, in 1927, been chief constable of Stalybridge, a post that also carried with it the rank of chief of the fire brigade. He had held that post for two years before taking up the appointment of chief superintendent in Sheffield.

In addition to the loss of Thomas Rawson, the brigade also saw one of its 'old stalwarts', Sergeant Albert Kennedy, who had joined the force in 1903, retire. His successor was the newly-promoted Sergeant George Hey, aged 31. He had only been in the force nine years, and was a graduate of the Institute of Fire Engineers. He was thought to be a natural replacement for Sergeant Kennedy.

The brigade's fleet now consisted of a Dennis pump escape (1915), a Dennis pump ladder (1920), a Leyland Metz TL (1930) and a Dennis Trailer Pump (1930). The chief constable, Mr May, recommended that the brigade man two appliances. He believed that this would be more advantageous for the borough, as when one pump was out on a call within the borough, there would always be another manned and ready to respond.

Although new to his post, the chief constable recommended to the Watch Committee in August that they purchase a further new pumping appliance. The cost of this was likely to be £1,550. He also recommended that a fire brigade mechanic be employed, but this the Committee rejected, stating that if a mechanic was required to attend to one of the engines, then the chief constable should call one in.

Following the chief constable's recommendation, on 26 April 1932, the brigade took possession of a new Dennis pump ladder, WN 4613. This was fitted with a White & Poppe six-cylinder petrol engine, and a 800 gallon per minute main turbine pump. It had an auxiliary 'first aid' pump for hose reels, and a 35ft Ajax extension ladder. The new engine's first call was to a fire at the British Ferro Tarmacadam Works, in Landore, on 3 May, but its first major fire was on 25 May 1932. It travelled to Gorseinon, some seven miles from Swansea, and the local press reported that 'travelling at speeds of up to 60 miles per hour on their new high powered engine, the Swansea Fire Brigade under Inspector Winteringham, arrived at the scene of a fire at the Station Hotel, Gorseinon, in under 10 minutes.'

The power of WN 4613 was again required on 20 June, when shortly after midnight, the brigade under Inspector Winteringham responded to a house fire in Clyndu Street in Morriston. On their arrival they were confronted with a blaze that was described as 'a roaring furnace,' and they were impeded by the sheer mass of people who had assembled from the neighbourhood. Some of these onlookers had carried out rescues before the fire brigade arrived. Unfortunately, a 16-year-old girl, Doreen Tanner, perished in the blaze, despite the efforts of her brother George to save her. One amazing rescue attempt, that was successful, was performed by a neighbour, Mr David Rees. While hanging on to a down pipe by one arm, he succeeded in lowering the dead girl's aunt, Mrs Roberts, the wife of the occupier, and young Colin Tanner, aged seven, to safety.

Inspector Francis Winteringham, who had joined the Swansea Brigade in October 1929 and had been involved in the reforms associated with Chief Constables Rawson and May, accepted the post of Superintendent in the Bristol City Fire Brigade and left the Swansea force in September 1931.

Chapter Seven

Tower Lane

One of the Swansea fire brigade's blackest days was Sunday 20 November 1932. At around 7am, a serious fire broke out at Llewellyn's Warehouse in the High Street, Swansea. The warehouse abutted a narrow thoroughfare known as Tower Lane, and the blaze was discovered by the caretaker of the Alexandra Road Chapel, a Mr Charles Stock. While on his way to open the chapel for the early morning service, he saw smoke coming from one of the warehouse's windows, about halfway down the lane. He investigated, then ran to the nearby fire station in Alexandra Road to raise the alarm.

On receiving the call, the brigade responded, under the command of Sergeant George Hey. Even though the fire station was only a stone's throw from the warehouse, it was clear when the brigade arrived that the fire had taken a complete hold of the premises. The lane was very narrow, only 10ft wide, and the the heat generated in the confined space made it impossible for the firemen to enter it. They had to fight the fire from two separate locations, in the High Street and Orchard Street. Both streets were roped off, as it was considered too dangerous for the crowds that had amassed to approach. The Mackworth Hotel, which was situated across the lane opposite the warehouse, was also affected by the blaze, which spread rapidly to damage some of the bedrooms and a bakery at the rear of the hotel. Although there was not thought to be any risk to life, the hotel was nonetheless evacuated. The warehouse fire had also spread to the company's garage, which

adjoined the warehouse. Throughout the fire explosions were heard, which were believed to be petrol tanks exploding in the garage.

The commemorative plaque at the Alexandra Road police station, a memorial to firemen Gethin Harris and Harold Bulley, who were killed at the Tower Lane fire on 20 November 1932. (Author's collection)

In order to combat the fire, the firemen did eventually enter the lane to direct their hose on the now rapidly spreading flames, in the hope of confining the blaze to the warehouse. While they were dragging the hose into position, the wall of Llewellyn's Warehouse collapsed, burying firemen Bulley, Harris and Drury. With no apparent thought for their own safety, firemen Morris, Jones and Rawlings rushed forward to rescue their colleagues. The scene that they were confronted with was one of absolute devastation. Fireman Drury's brass helmet was on the ground, totally crushed and distorted. In what was described as 'a frenzied rescue' the three firemen began to remove the red hot debris so that their comrades could be extricated. All that could be seen of Fireman Harris was his head and eyes, and at that time he was reported to be conscious. Fireman Morris's hands were badly burnt as he removed the debris, but this did not stop him from continuing to try and rescue the trapped firemen. Eventually all three men were pulled from the rubble.

Immediately after the collapse of the wall, Chief Constable May ordered all the remaining firemen to withdraw from the building. This was a fortunate decision, as the roof soon collapsed. The brigade continued to battle with the blaze from outside the building for a further 10 hours, and they managed to save the adjoining premises.

All the injured firemen were taken to Swansea General Hospital. Fireman Gethin Harris, who had a good physique, because of his interest in boxing and wrestling, was the most seriously injured, although it was thought that he would eventually make a full recovery. However, he tragically died of his injuries on the morning of 22 November. Aged 27, Fireman Harris had joined the borough force in December 1926. He was unmarried and lived with his parents at 'The Cottage' in Wern Road, Landore. His injured colleague, Fireman William Drury, was considered to be 'getting on well' and Fireman Harold Bulley was described as 'much the same.'

Fireman Gethin Harris was buried on Friday 25 November, with a 'full service' funeral. His body travelled on the brigade's recently purchased Dennis fire engine WN 4613, and proceeded from his home in Landore on a route that took the cortège past the Alexandra Road police fire brigade station, down St

The Swansea fire brigade with their new Leyland Metz 85ft turntable ladder. The principle officer is believed to be Chief Constable Thomas Rawson. Next to the civilian is Sergeant George Charles Hey; top right of the photograph is Harold Bulley and front row second left is Gethin Harris, both of whom died as a result of injuries sustained at the Tower Lane fire on 20 November 1932. Second row, fourth from the left, is Frederick Waters. (Swansea fire brigade)

The funeral cortage of Fireman Gethin Harris, passing through Landore en route to Oystermouth Cemetery, Mumbles, on 25 November 1932.

Helen's Road, where it passed the hospital before arriving at the Oystermouth cemetery in the Mumbles. The funeral, which was attended by representatives of many brigades, including the previous inspector, Francis Winteringham, with a contingent from the Bristol City Fire Brigade. Those that had followed the cortège had marched from Landore through the town to the 'Slip Bridge', where they boarded buses to take them to the cemetery.

While the cortège was travelling down St Helen's Road, Fireman Bulley insisted to be taken on to the hospital's balcony to see his close friend's funeral procession pass. His fiancée, Miss Maude Thomas, attributed this excursion to his relapse, which led to his death from septicaemia on Monday 28 November, aged 26. Harold Robert Bulley had joined

the Swansea force in 1929. He had been due to complete his 'living in period' at the police station in three weeks time, and was then to get married. On the evening of Wednesday 30 November, a large crowd gathered at Swansea's High Street Railway Station, and the body of Fireman Bulley was placed aboard a train to be taken back to his place of birth for burial. The coffin was draped in a Union flag and accompanied to Norwich by Detective Inspector William Francis.

The chief constable, F.J. May, read out a report on the warehouse fire at the following month's Watch Committee meeting, in which he recommended that firemen 74 Hugh Rawlings, 152 Frederick Hollister Morris, and 124 Ebenezer Jones be commended for their courageous conduct at the fire. As a result of this, all three firemen were awarded the Royal Humane Society for the Protection of Life from Fire Bronze Medal. For Frederick Morris, this award was to be in the form of a bar, as he had already been awarded the medal after the Wassail Square fire in 1930.

As a memorial to the two firemen that lost their lives, Gethin Harris and Harold Bulley, a bronze plaque was mounted on a wall in the Alexandra Road police fire brigade station in November 1936, where it hangs to this day.

Following the death of Firemen Gethin Harris, his aged parents had been repaid his superannuation deductions at 15 shillings a week. Just two years later, these payments ceased. Although this followed the letter of the law regarding an unmarried man's pension, the Swansea Watch Committee believed that because of the exceptional circumstances, the Corporation should look into the matter. Whether this enquiry led to any further payments being made was not reported.

January 1933 saw the appointment of a new inspector of the Swansea Fire Brigade, Martin Chadwick, aged 32. He was an associate member of the Institute of Fire Engineers, and commenced his duties at the central fire brigade station. Inspector Chadwick joined Swansea from the Kettering fire brigade, and succeeded Inspector Winteringham, who had secured the post of superintendent of the Bristol City Fire Brigade some months earlier.

Inspector Chadwick's baptism of fire came on the evening of Thursday 26 January, when a fire occurred at Weaver's Flour Mill. Happily, the fire was not as serious as the devastating fire at Weaver's in June 1926, which was one of the worst disasters in the history of the town. This time, however, the brigade were seriously hampered by the arctic conditions. The water and spray from the jets froze on the surface of the roads, and on the firemen's uniforms. The turntable ladder, which was used as a water tower, proved indispensable, permitting the jets to be directed into the most inaccessible of places.

The efficiency of the brigade's latest acquisition, WN 4613, was put to the test, when at around 4.45am on Tuesday 10 October, after a period of torrential rain, an underground tunnel, which was part of the new surface water and sewerage system in Neath Road, Landore, became flooded. Nine workmen were trapped, but fortunately they were working behind a air-tight door, which was held closed by the pressure of water. The level of water within the tunnel had risen sharply as a result of the surface drainage, and rapidly reached a height of six feet, which imprisoned the men behind the air-tight door. A large number of onlookers gathered, most of whom were awakened by the arrival of the fire brigade.

In order to assess the situation, Chief Constable May, Inspector Chadwick and Sergeant Hey, along with Firemen Ferguson and Speight, were lowered some 30ft into the tunnel by means of a workmen's cage. Once at the bottom, they set in the pump. After some two hours of pumping, the water level was sufficiently reduced to allow the workmen to walk out unaided, none the worse for their ordeal.

Further additions were made to the brigade's efficiency when oxygen breathing apparatus sets were purchased. These were put to good use on 4 November 1933, when at 4.35am the brigade took two pumps to a call, under the command of Inspector Chadwick. The fire was at No.44 King Edward's Road, Swansea, in the lower part of the town near Victoria Park. When the brigade arrived they saw that the building was completely smoke-logged. Inspector Chadwick and other members of the brigade immediately donned the new breathing apparatus and entered the building. They searched it to see whether anyone was trapped inside. Thankfully, no one was, although the firemen did rescue an old greyhound dog, which had been overcome by the smoke.

Like Swansea, the town of Carmarthen was engaged in discussion with outlying districts about the annual cost of providing fire cover. On the morning of Saturday 6 January 1934, at around 10.30am, a serious fire occurred at the Farmers Co-operative Stores in St Clears, approximately nine miles from Carmarthen. No final decision had been made about fire cover, and as a result the Carmarthen brigade did not attend the call. The alarm was then raised at the Tenby, Haverfordwest and Swansea fire brigades. First on the scene was the Haverfordwest brigade, which had travelled 21 miles, then moments later the Tenby brigade arrived, having covered 18 miles. Finally, the Swansea brigade, with Inspector Chadwick in charge, arrived after covering 35 miles in record time, around 45 minutes.

While en route to the fire, the Swansea engine met a local police officer at Carmarthen bridge, who mounted the appliance and directed the driver to St Clears. After the fire, the police officer was asked if he needed a lift back to Carmarthen, but he declined 'on health grounds,' an observation on Fireman Speight's remarkable driving.

Although the Gower and Lwchwr District Councils had apparently accepted the Swansea council's terms, relating to fire cover in their respective areas, the same could not be said of the Pontardawe and Ystradgynlais councils in the Swansea Valley. Following a serious fire at a garage in Capel Road, Clydach, the garage man-ager wrote in the local newspaper 'During early hours of Saturday morning last (13 April 1935) we were unfortunate enough to have an outbreak of fire in our Capel Road garage, resulting in one vehicle becoming a total loss, and several other vehicles being severely damaged.'

The local police had apparently requested the assistance of the

Swansea and other fire brigades, but no help had been forthcoming. Negotiations between the councils had broken down in September 1933, when the Pontardawe council failed to agree the terms offered by Swansea, deciding that it would look into establishing its own fire brigade, which it duly did. In 1935, the new Ystradgynlais council fire brigade reportedly attended a fire at a farm in Abercrave. In 1936 the Pontardawe council, having purchased a Leyland fire engine with a 400 gallon per minute pump and other equipment, at a cost of £1,920, officially opened its own fire station. Sidney Fennel was captain of the brigade.

The chief constable expressed the need for a further fire appliance and improved accommodation for the fire brigade at the January 1935 Watch Committee meeting. The engine would be a replacement for the brigade's oldest appliance. As for the accommodation, five out of 12 permanent firemen lived a considerable distance from the station, and full use could not be made of their services. He further remarked that the time had come for a full-time, permanent staff to be appointed for the fire brigade, and a new fire station should be erected, with the view to accommodating the staff in, or near to, the station.

In May the chief constable's recommendations were accepted, although the council added the proviso that the adoption of the recommendations in no way committed the council to the scheme. Since 1870 Swansea had

PC Frederick Hollister Morris was awarded the Royal Society for the Protection of Life from Fire Medal on two occasions, first after the Wassail Square fire in March 1930, and then for his part in attempting to rescue his colleagues, Firemen Bulley and Harris, in 1932. (Mr F. Morris, son)

Swansea borough police fire brigade appliance and crew after extinguishing a fire at the Mannersman Tube Works, Landore, c.1930.

had six 'fire stations', three of which were no more than sheds to house the manual engines. The two stations at Goat Street and Pleasant Street were really built to accommodate fire engines, although they suffered from a lack of accommodation and stable space from the time they were built. Alexandra Road, with its three-bay appliance room, was also beginning to be too small.

In September 1936, one of the two recommendations made by the chief constable was acted on. A new Dennis Braidwood 'Big 6' pump escape fire engine, ACY 463 was purchased. It was of a design that had been adopted by the London Fire Brigade, and the crew had safer seating. A transverse cross-sectional seat allowed the firemen to sit alongside and behind the driver, whereas on earlier appliances the crew had had to sit along the sides, a dangerous practice which had led to firemen falling off and sustaining serious injuries, or even death. The new engine was Swansea's first of the type, and was powered by a six-cylinder Meadows petrol engine. It had a 1000 gallon per minute pump, and a demountable 50ft Morris escape ladder. Its baptism came at a fire at a printers shop in Bellevue Street on 1 October.

The chief constable's other recommendation, for new premises for the fire brigade, was deferred.

At the annual Swansea police dinner, which was

Swansea fire brigade's Dennis pump WN 4613, pictured after a fire call to the Co-operative Stores at St Clear's, near Carmarthen, on 6 January 1934. The officer in charge is Inspector Martin Chadwick, and Fireman Speight is in the driver's seat. (South Wales Police Museum, curator Jeremy Glenn)

held at the Mackworth Hotel on Wednesday 13 January 1937, the chairman of the Watch Committee, Councillor George Edwards, dismissed any proposals for a new central police fire brigade station. He did, however, express the view that the present station was not large enough to accommodate both the police and the fire brigade.

As rumours of war in Europe began to be heard, the British Government introduced the Air Raid Precautions Act in 1937. This placed on local authorities the duty of preparing and carrying out effective schemes for the passive defence of their area against aerial attack. When planning their fire cover authorities had to bear in mind that in the event of high explosive and incendiary attacks from the air, large numbers of small fires would occur more or less simultaneously. The normal peace time resources of the brigade would be unable to deal with this type of situation. Therefore it was of vital importance that Swansea's fire brigade be extended.

The solution was though to be the enrolment and training of large numbers of auxiliaries. In 1938, Swansea employed both full and part-time auxiliary personnel, as received Home Office issued appliances and equipment. The first consignment consisted of

16 trailer pumps, which could be easily manoeuvred into position by a relatively small number of men, usually two. Their other advantage was that they could be easily attached to the back of a small van or family saloon car and towed to the scene of a fire. This led to the emergence of many varied and strange vehicles being used in the fire service, most of which were specially adapted domestic vehicles.

The chief constable reported to the Watch Committee in 1938 that in order to meet the requirements of the Air Raid Precautions scheme, Swansea would require around 200 special constables, along with a substantial number of personnel for the auxiliary services, air raid wardens, firemen and ambulance drivers. The committee granted the chief constable the power to advertise for volunteers.

While in the throes of making the necessary changes to ready the brigade for war, the chief constable lost his fire chief, Inspector Martin Chadwick. The inspector was a native of Jarrow in the north-east, and he accepted the post of superintendent of the Newcastle-upon-Tyne fire brigade, which he had first joined as a young police fireman in February 1923. In July, Inspector Chadwick's replacement was announced. Ironically, his successor was Sergeant Errington McKinnell, aged 34. He, like Inspector Chadwick, had joined the

Swansea fire brigade's new Dennis 'Big 6' pump escape outside the Alexandra Road fire station on 22 September 1936. Inspector Martin Chadwick is in the driving seat. (Edwin Brimble)

The Dennis 'Big 6' prior to leaving the Dennis factory in Guildford for delivery to Swansea. (Surrey County Council)

Newcastle-upon-Tyne fire brigade in 1923, and was an associate member of the Institute of Fire Engineers, as well as being a fully qualified Home Office ARP Instructor. The Swansea Watch Committee thought him 'ideally suited for the post'.

An important feature of the fireman's uniform, not only in Swansea, but also in other fire brigades was the brass helmet. It disappeared in 1938, to be replaced by the less ornate, but safer, black leather helmet. The reason for the change was that firemen had been injured in accidents while attending fires, often when electric cables came into contact with the brass helmet. One such accident, which had tragic results, was at a fire in Parkstone, Dorset. Fireman Frank Phillips, aged 29, suffered an electric shock and died. His brother, who was attending the same fire, also suffered an electric shock, but thankfully recovered.

Firemen Charlie Millis, Ted Lodge and Frank Usher on the roof of the Alexandra Road fire station.

As large numbers of auxiliary personnel attended the Alexandra Road station for training, the chief constable again remarked on the cramped conditions. He informed the Watch Committee that a new station would cost £40,000 to £50,000, with the work and cost extended over 1939 to 1941. He thought that although the idea of a new station had been abandoned a year ago on financial grounds, the time had now come to tackle the problem. In his belief it would not be long before Swansea would have to employ more permanent firemen instead of relying on auxiliary firemen (off-duty policemen who assisted the regular firemen).

In 1938 Swansea already had a large number of auxiliary fire service personnel, who were employed to assist the local brigade after the 1937 Act. In October these auxiliaries were given a 'test call' to a fire at the King's Dock as part of their initial training. They responded with their trailer pumps, towed by the 'Black Maria' and the Swansea fire brigade's newly-acquired Bedford Limousine fire tender, which was also equipped with a radio. However, the radio was only 'one way', so although the controller at the central station could pass information to the officer in charge, they could never be certain that he had received it. In order to comply with the 1937 Act,

it was thought that Swansea would require 22 trailer pumps and around 70 appliances for use throughout the district, as well as around 500 personnel, consisting of fully-trained men, women auxiliaries and messengers. The latter were specially trained scouts.

The first report of auxiliaries assisting the brigade was made on 13 December 1938, when they attended a fire at the Vetch Field's East Stand. The fire occurred

Also on the roof at Alexandra Road are (standing, left to right): Police Firemen Jim Davies, Edgar West, Bill Parker and Eddie Chambers. Charlie Millis and Frank Usher are seated.

a little after 8pm, while AFS personnel were attending drills and training at the central police station. They accompanied the brigade to the fire, and according to the chief constable, 'worked admirably throughout'.

Swansea's first Home Office issued vehicle was a Fordson (CCY 788), which apart from conveying personnel, was fitted with a 'heavy pump' for use in

Swansea fire brigade with the Dennis pump in the rear yard of the Alexandra Road fire station. The photograph is believed to date from 1938, as the uniform and leather helmets were brought in after the brass helmets were discontinued.

his secondment was Acting Inspector George Hey.

Also, in April, the chief constable informed the Watch Committee that provision had been made in the programme of capital works for the erection of a new fire station. In addition, under the emergency fire brigade organisation, he recommended that the old police station at Morriston and Sketty church hall be made available as auxiliary fire stations. The Morriston police station, which had been declared surplus to requirements by Chief Constable Rawson in April 1930 and at one point had been suggested as a centre for the unemployed, was now returning to its original function as a fire station.

water relays. It was painted in a colour that was to become the signature colour of all AFS and NFS fire appliances throughout the war, 'battleship grey'.

Inspector McKinnell, although he had only been in charge of the brigade since July 1938, was seconded to the Home Office as a temporary fire brigade instructor in April 1939. Although working away at the Home Office, he remained attached to the Swansea brigade. His replacement for the duration of

Chapter Eight

The War Years

With Britain at war, the Swansea contingent of the auxiliary fire service was still in training. That training was put to the test in the early hours of Saturday 21 October 1939, when at around 3am the entire premises of Marks & Spencer, in Oxford Street and through to Park Street, including a recently built extension, were completely destroyed by fire, along with the premises of Jenkins & Co. Ironmongers.

The Swansea fire brigade turned out, assisted by the Fisher Street AFS station. Even with the brigade's turntable ladder, an ample supply of water and several jets in position, it was soon clear that further help was needed to combat the huge blaze. All the town's AFS units were mobilised. There were, unfortunately, casualties among the firefighters. Auxiliary fireman Thomas Ashley, a Townhill

member of the Gwent Road AFS station, was seriously injured when their pump overturned coming down Mount Pleasant Hill. His leg was virtually severed and had to be amputated. Acting Inspector George Hey and Fireman Idwal Davies were overcome by fumes and taken to Swansea hospital, where they remained for a few days.

Mumbles AFS personnel with their pump at Underhill Park, Mumbles, 1939. (Mrs Wendy Cope)

At the height of the fire, people living in Park Street were ordered to vacate their homes. They were taken to the safety of the nearby Park Buildings. So fierce was the fire that it was considered a great achievement on the part of the firefighters that they prevented the blaze from spreading further along the block.

Despite the initial hopes of success of the chief constable and Acting Inspector Hey, who had been directing operations, at around 4.20am huge flames suddenly appeared, and it became obvious that the

Auxiliary Fire Service firemen and women outside the Southend fire station, Mumbles, c.1940.

Personnel at the Fisher Street Auxiliary fire station in 1940. It was bombed out during the war, and 10 fire service personnel were injured. (Mrs Anita Jackson)

blaze had taken a far more serious hold. The brigade had set in to hydrants from the surrounding streets, and from vantage points from the roof of Edward's Buildings opposite, directed their jets onto the flames. The turntable ladder was in use as a water tower. An indication of the severity of the outbreak was that although the call was received at around 3am, the firemen were still fighting the blaze until well after 7am, and only then did it begin to show signs of abating. The height of the frontage of Marks & Spencer had been 99ft in Oxford Street and 112ft in Park Street, and the depth of the store was 160ft. The whole of this area was completely destroyed, and the damage was estimated at £250,000.

The chief constable, in a statement made after the fire, congratulated the AFS personnel who had attended the fire, saying that 'his only concern was to prevent their zeal and enthusiasm in order that it would not lead to casualties'. He reported that 28 regular members of the fire brigade, 20 police and 135 members of the AFS had attended the fire.

At a dinner for the Guildhall's part-time AFS personnel on 22 February 1940, Alderman Morris informed all those present in his speech that Swansea had 406 AFS members, all of whom had attended a specially convened test. There were, he stressed, sufficient men to man every pump that was available to Swansea.

After the Marks & Spencer fire in October 1939, the Swansea brigade was only required to attend minor outbreaks of fire. Even the town's first air raid, which took place on Thursday 27 June 1940, caused little damage. The raid began at 3.30am. Bombs were dropped on Kilvey Hill and Danygraig Road, some of which failed to detonate.

The chief constable proposed a revised scheme of

The Pontardawe Urban District fire brigade with their Leyland pump, 1940. While working in Swansea during the February Blitz, two of its members were killed and another seriously injured. Their pump was also destroyed. (Mr Keith Evans)

AFS arrangements in October 1939, which provided for a reduction of full-time AFS firemen to 192 and part-time firemen to 220, which would reduce costs from £78,000 to £28,000. In April the Home Secretary approved the scheme. A further cost-cutting measure was agreed by the committee. There were 24 constables at the central police station, who

The fireman on the right is Edward 'Ted' Evans who, as part of the Pontardawe crew, was severely injured on the night of 22 February 1941. He lost an eye and suffered crush injuries. The fireman on his right is Walter Gough. (Mrs Joan Phillips)

in addition to performing their usual street duties, were also required to standby for fire duties. For this they were paid a non-pensionable allowance of 3s a week. After reviewing the arrangements, in view of the availability of full and part-time AFS personnel, the chief constable recommended that this practice be discontinued, saving £1,250 per year.

Chief Constable May became eligible for retirement in May, having completed 26 years service. However, under the terms of an Act of 1939, councils could retain the services of police, firemen and others during the state of emergency. The chief constable was still only 46 years old, which some councillors thought 'was to young to retire'.

Throughout 1940 Swansea was the target of air raids, most of which resulted in light damage. On the night of 1 September, Swansea experienced its first Blitz-type raid, when a large number of German aircraft dropped around 251 high explosive bombs and 1,000 incendiary bombs on the town, killing 33 people and seriously injuring 36.

On 17 January 1941, a second Blitz-type air raid was launched on Swansea. Around 100 high explosive bombs, and 6–7,000 incendiary bombs were dropped, killing 55 people and seriously injuring 38. Serious damage was caused to various parts of the town.

The local newspaper published stories of deeds of heroism and courage that had been performed by members of the public, ARP personnel and the police, fire brigade and AFS. All were commended for their devotion to duty and tireless efforts in combating the fires that broke out when the bombs were dropped.

The 21 Fire Force NFS, pictured following a drill competition in 1943. Second from the right (seated) is Jack Fox, who went on to be Deputy Chief Fire Officer of the Swansea fire brigade. (Mr Alan Fox)

Swansea's 'Three-night Blitz' has been well documented in the book of that name by John Alban. No amount of training could have prepared Swansea's firefighters for what they were confronted with on the nights of the 19, 20 and 21 February 1941. For more than 13 hours each night, over 800 high explosive bombs and 30,000 incendiary bombs were dropped on the town. Two hundred and thirty

Emergency water pipes being unloaded ready for the installation of water mains. (Mr Alan Fox)

people were killed, and 232 injured. It was described as the worst catastrophe the town had ever known.

The severity of the bombing and the ensuing fires meant that fire crews travelled from fire to fire. Some firemen were away from home for the whole three days, and some, sadly, were never to return. On Thursday 20 February, following an explosion at Teilo Crescent in the town's Mayhill district, AFS Fireman Herbert Reginald Daniels was killed.

At the same incident, Section Leader George Hughes and Samuel Williams, after inspecting the bombed-out houses, came across a man who was trapped beneath the rubble. Working below a wall that was in danger of collapsing, the two men succeeded in extricating the man, sadly only to find that he had died. For this rescue, the two firefighters were awarded a badge for brave conduct, a laurel leaf and a citation for bravery.

With Swansea's firefighters stretched to the full, assistance was given by outside AFS units. One such unit was from the Pontardawe Urban District Council. This unit was attending a fire in a clothing establishment in the Strand, when a bomb struck a building near them, which subsequently collapsed and buried the firemen and their appliance. AFS

NFS firemen engaged in laying new emergency water mains. (Mr Alan Fox)

Firemen Daniel Winston Davies, from Brynamman, and Herbert Lewis, from Cwmgorse, were killed, and their colleague, Edward 'Ted' Evans, suffered serious crush injuries and lost an eye. The bodies of both firemen could not be retrieved from the rubble until six days later.

A Bedford emergency dam-laying lorry, one of several NFS appliances stationed at Swansea during the war. (Mr Alan Fox)

The AFS Station in St Michael's Church Hall, in Bohun Street, Manselton, was hit by an incendiary bomb. Fortunately only minor damage was done, and the fire was extinguished by the on-duty firemen using stirrup pumps. Another incident occurred when the Fisher Street station, situated near the bottom of Salubrious Passage, took a direct hit. The building was totally destroyed, and 10 AFS on-duty personnel were injured.

At the beginning of the war, there had been some

1,400 local authority fire brigades in England and Wales, and around 185 brigades in Scotland. There were also a handful of district brigades that only operated within their own boundary. The various brigades had a vast number of differing types of equipment, from the most modern engines to steamers and even manual engines. When the full impact of the Blitz hit some British towns in 1940, and the local authority brigades and the AFS had to deal with fires on a scale that had never been envisaged, it became apparent that the peacetime methods of firefighting were inadequate. On 18 August 1941, the National Fire Service (NFS) was established. AFS members changed their buttons and badges to NFS, and appliances and equipment were standardised. Most of the AFS ad hoc vehicles for towing were phased out, to be replaced by purpose-built appliances. Swansea formed part of what became the Fire Force 21 area.

This photograph shows the ingenuity used during the AFS years prior to August 1941. A Triumph family saloon is converted for fire brigade use. (Swansea Archives, the Guildhall)

Along with the NFS came an array of appliances, most of which were on the standard bus and lorry chassis. One such appliance was the Leyland Titan 100ft turntable ladder, which served Swansea's brigade until 1963. Other engines towed a range of trailer pumps, which became the backbone of the fire service. Their versatility and easy handling enabled them to be manoeuvred into quite inaccessible locations, invaluable when many roads and streets had become impassable. To accommodate these

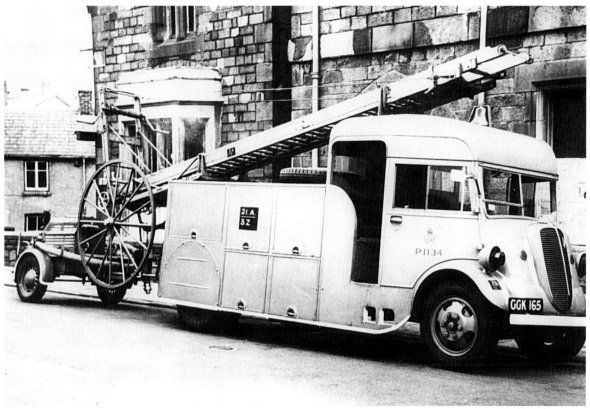

An NFS Fordson pump escape towing a trailer pump, seen here outside the old Martin Street fire station, Morriston, during World War Two. (Mr Alan Fox)

An Austin auxiliary towing vehicle (ATV), a type used in large numbers during the war for the towing and transportation of personnel. (Mr Alan Fox)

Swansea fire brigade's first motorised fire engine, originally a pump escape. It underwent body refurbishment, which resulted in it being used as a pump, not an escape. This photograph was taken at the Derwen Fawr Water Depot, during the war. (Surrey County Council)

appliances a water supply headquarters depot was opened at Derwen Fawr, near Sketty.

During the first two years of their existence, the AFS at Swansea had been at the forefront of the town's firefighting during the periods of the worst bombing. The NFS, however, although it consisted of former AFS firemen, did not experience the same intensity of action. After the three-night Blitz, Swansea suffered no more such raids until 16 February 1943, when a raid commenced at around 10pm that lasted

Looking up Wind Street, Swansea, at AFS firemen damping down the smouldering remains of the Ben Evans department store, Castle Square, 1941. (South Wales Evening Post)

AFS firemen engaged in firefighting at the Ben Evans store, 1941.
(South Wales Evening Post)

NFS drill exercises at South Prospect Place in the Strand, 1942. (South Wales Evening Post)

A well-earned tea break for NFS firemen in 1942. (South Wales Evening Post)

Some of the fire appliances that were stationed at Derwen Fawr Depot during the war. (Mr Alan Fox)

less than an hour. Thirty-two high explosive and phosphorous bombs were dropped on the town, one of which fell near the entrance to the Swansea General Hospital, forcing the evacuation of the patients. Thirty-four people were killed and 58 seriously injured.

The NFS existed throughout the remainder of the war and into the post-war years until 1 April 1948, when control of fire brigades was returned to local authorities. After the war, fire brigades saw a reduction in the stations, personnel and equipment that had been necessary during the war. Most of the fire appliances were handed over to local authority brigades, and some were used well into the 1950s and 1960s. In addition to this, brigades saw a large intake of recruits, most of whom were ex-service personnel from the armed forces. Others were NFS members who transferred over.

Under the terms of the Fire Services Act, brigades were responsible for:

Two photographs of Castle Street, Swansea, before and after the bombing raids of 1941. (Mr Alan Fox)

AFS personnel in the bombed-out remains of Swansea Market. (South Wales Evening Post)

AFS personnel posing for a photograph outside Pressdee's Funeral Parlour, Stanley Place, Mumbles. The funeral parlour was used as an emergency fire station during the war. (Mrs Wendy Cope)

The provision of men and equipment (most appliances and equipment in use with local authority brigades were ex-Home Office issue from NFS days).

Training personnel.

Making arrangements for dealing with fires.

Obtaining information on buildings and property for fire-fighting purposes.

Mitigating damage resulting from fires, and giving fire prevention advice.

There was also provision for brigades assisting each other at fires under a 'mutual aid scheme'. The Swansea brigade had already done this on many occasions, but now there would be no argument or delay in turning out to a fire, as had

AFS personnel outside Pressdee's Funeral Parlour, Mumbles. (Mr Alan Fox)

Personnel of 21 Fire Force outside Swansea Guildhall, 1942. (Mr Don Ralph, deceased)

AFS firemen and women outside the Southend fire station, Mumbles, during the war.

Male and female members of the National Fire Service outside the National Training College in Brighton. (Mr Alan Fox)

been the case in the past before payment had been agreed.

For the first time, apart from a four-year period from 1858 to 1862, the fire brigade was totally separate from the police. The Watch Committee had to select a chief fire officer, which led to the appointment of William Frederick Redman. He was from Bristol and had served in the NFS throughout the war as an assistant fire force commander with the No.7 Region. His deputy was Swansea-born Leonard Oliver Clarke, who, like Mr Redman, had seen wartime service with the NFS and the Home Office, as well as being a senior staff officer in the Fire Force 21 area.

Chapter Nine

A New Era

The new brigade had three stations. The Alexandra Road, or central station, which in June 1935 the then chief constable had recommended be replaced, was still in service despite the fact that the council had agreed the building of new accommodation. By 1948 the fire brigade comprised 81 officers and men, including three part-time firemen at Mumbles, and an immediate remedy was required. The Home Office agreed that a new station/headquarters was required, and an interim measure had to found. This was achieved by accommodating stores and personnel at the aptly-named Dennis Hotel, which was situated at the junction of Orchard Street and Alexandra Road, diagonally opposite the Alexandra

NFS recruits pictured in 1946. Some of the personnel photographed here went on to serve with the Swansea fire brigade for many years. They included Arthur Edwards, Jack 'Sailor' Fenwick, Dennis 'Dapper' Davies, Colin John, Bert Jeffers and Lew Edwards. (Gregory Davies, son Dennis Davies, ex-SFB)

Road police station (later to become Lloyds Bank). One problem with this arrangement was that when a call was received, the firemen had to run across the main road to board the engine.

The brigade's shift pattern at this time was a 96-hour week, worked on a two-shift system of 24 hours on, 24 hours off. This then changed to a 60-hour working week until the mid 1950s, when a 56-hour week was devised.

One of Swansea's other stations was Sub Station 1, Southend, Mumbles, which was an old green corrugated tin sheet shed used to house fire appliances during the war, with accommodation for only two appliances at first. Accommodation for on-duty personnel was provided at the 'Coast House' near the George Hotel, although later in 1948

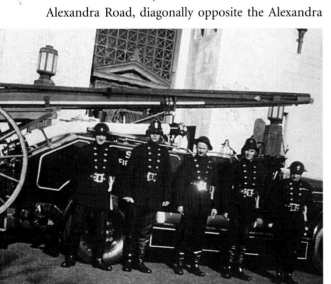

Members of Swansea fire brigade after the 1948 reorganisation. Only three of the five firemen pictured here have been identified. From the right are Alfie Boyle, John Carey and Vic Ockwell. (Mrs Wendy Cope)

accommodation was added to the existing appliance room. At the time of the change over the Swansea fire brigade had three ex-NFS members stay on at the Mumbles as part-time firemen.

The provision of a station at Morriston had not been possible early in 1948. Alterations were ongoing to the old Martin Street police station, which was being coverted for fire brigade use. Later that year the work was completed and the station became operational.

Swansea's fleet of appliances at this time consisted of:

Central:

1 Dennis Major pump, WN 4613

1 Bedford pump, FYH 125 (ex-NFS)

1 Leyland Titan 100ft turntable ladder GLW 429 (ex-NFS)

1 Pump salvage tender

1 Emergency tender

1 Foam tender/pump

1 Austin towing vehicle and trailer pump GLR 951 (ex-NFS)

Headquarters:

2 Staff cars

1 Wireless car

1 Motor cycle combination, GLD 163

Mumbles:

1 Ford heavy pump unit, GXM 325 (ex-NFS)

1 Dennis Major pump, ACY 463

Morriston:

1 Fordson pump escape, GGK 165 and portable Coventry climax pump

By 1950 the brigade's strength had risen from 81 to 94 and still included three part-time firemen. These were eventually phased out in the early 1950s.

From 1949 onwards, possible sites for a new fire brigade headquarters were investigated. Eventually the site of an old

house, 'The Laurels' in Grove Place was chosen. Also on the site were an old cottage, 'Tyn yr Graig', and some bomb-damaged houses. The whole area was considered for compulsory purchase.

Above and below: *Pictured with the Leyland Titan Merryweather 100ft turntable ladder in Richards Street, Swansea in 1949, are firemen Harry Jones and Harry Davies.* (Swansea fire brigade)

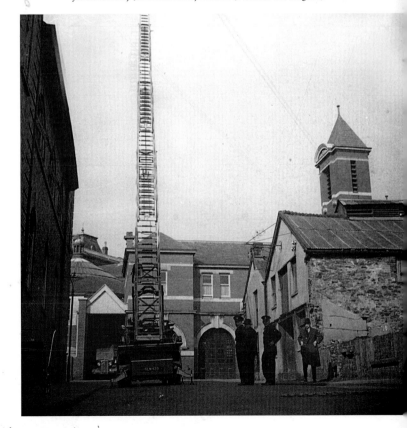

Firemen Harry Jones and Harry Davies. (Swansea fire brigade)

GLW 429

Fireman Chris Wade with the Dennis pump WN 4613, in the Alexandra Road fire station yard in 1949.

In 1949 the government proposed to include an auxiliary fire service as part of its civil defence structure. This would mean that local unpaid volunteers would attend fire stations for instruction and training. In Swansea there was a lack of recruits, and training sessions were not well attended.

The fire brigade were now not only responsible for fires, but also for incidents or accidents that required

A 1948 photograph of Swansea fire brigade personnel from the Mumbles station, most of whom were among the only part-time firemen retained by the brigade. Their numbers eventually dwindled to three before being wound-up in the mid-1950s. (Mrs Wendy Cope)

rescue or extrication of members of the public or others. One such incident that the brigade attended was in January 1950, when they were called to release the body of Evan Davies, who had been run over by the Mumbles train near the Patti Pavilion.

On Saturday 9 September 1950 a major disaster resulting in tragic deaths occurred in Swansea. Just before 6am, houses 24, 25 and 26 on Prince of Wales Road collapsed on to a scrap yard and stables in the upper Strand, killing seven people.

There had been a previous subsidence in March 1914, which involved numbers 17 to 20 Prince of Wales Road. The rear garden walls and a large retaining wall, which loomed over three cottages below, numbers 21, 22 and 23 Flint Mill Row, crashed down on to the three dwellings. Fortunately, the collapse occurred at around 4pm in the afternoon, giving the residents in Flint Mill Row time to escape. Although no one had been killed or injured, three houses were reduced to a mass of debris. Twenty-five people were made homeless. When the incident was

An ex-NFS Bedford fire engine that went on to serve Swansea fire brigade until 1951, seen here at the Southend fire station, Mumbles. (Mrs Mary Kostromin)

Swansea fire brigade football team in 1948, pictured before their away game against the Cardiff fire brigade. Back row (left to right, players only): B. Davies, W. Edwards, C. Jones, J. Scott, A. Davies, J. Jones. Front row: E. Stratton, L. Harries, J. Rippon, J. Beare and B. Williams. Supporters (from the left) are W. Lewis, J. Farley, H. Davies, L. Edwards, G.H. Davies, G. Jones, S. Rees, Morgan, J. Carey, D. Thomas, F. Trew and G. Petherick. (Alan Davies)

reported in the local press in 1914, another previous subsidence was alluded to in the same vicinity, which killed a horse in the stable below.

In the days leading up to Saturday 9 September, the emergency services, especially the fire brigade, had been busy with severe flooding throughout the town, after the worst rain in Swansea for years. On their arrival in Prince of Wales Road, they were confronted with scenes reminiscent of the Blitz. The fronts of the houses looked practically unscathed, but the same could not be said of the rear, as walls, roofs, floors and all the contents had collapsed into the

Strand below. The houses were home to 23 people, nearly all of whom were in bed when the collapse occurred.

The emergency services, along with neighbours and council workers, were involved in protracted rescues. Three people were dead and five were still unaccounted for. A mass of debris, including furniture and rubble, had to be moved by hand to locate those missing. Weather conditions were poor. The rescuers worked throughout the morning and well into the day, and finally retrieved all those missing. The death toll for the morning stood at seven, and 15 injured people were taken to the hospital. Eleven of these were detained. One woman had a particularly lucky escape. She was seen walking out of the rubble in her night-dress, relatively unscathed. The seven people killed were:

Marlene Morgan, aged six years
Desmond Morgan, aged eight years
Roger Morgan, aged three years
Cyril Stanley Lewis, aged 30 years
Marilyn Lewis, aged eight years
William Lewis, aged five years
Samuel Belkin, aged 74 years

The Dennis Hotel at the junction of Alexandra Road and Orchard Street. Following its use as an hotel, it became Lloyds Bank. (Swansea Reference Library)

Two views of the Alexandra Road police fire station, from where the Dennis Hotel once stood. In the second photograph the bricked-up doorways of the appliance bay rooms can be seen. (Author's collection)

Another view of the Dennis Hotel. For a while the hotel was used as accommodation for off-duty firemen.

At the inquest it was explained that the houses, which had been built in the 1890s, stood on what can only be described as a viaduct. Due to the nature of the foundations, the houses had been slowly sinking over the years, and it was believed that the disaster occurred as a result of the collapse of one of the viaduct's arches.

Swansea, as a seaport, was always at risk of ship fires. On Friday 2 February 1951, a serious incident that resulted in loss of life occurred at the docks.

At 5am on Friday morning a series of explosions rocked Swansea Docks, sending shock waves as far afield as Port Talbot. The oil tanker, the MV *Atlantic Duchess*, which had put into Swansea two days earlier after her maiden voyage with a consignment of oil from Abadan, in the Persian Gulf, and discharged her cargo of 12,100 tons of butanized oil, exploded, broke in two and ignited.

Swansea fire control received the call from the Queen's Dock gatehouse, informing them of the fire at No.2 jetty, at 5am. The brigade responded with two Major pumps, one emergency tender and a foam tender towing a trailer pump. Station Officer Jack Fox was in charge. Under the terms of the mutual aid agreement, pumps attended from Morriston, Pontardulais, Neath and Pontardawe, from the Glamorgan county brigade. Despite these additional pumps, at 6am a 'brigade call' "Smokey" was put out. This was a request for off-duty personnel Colleried to attend the fire, and 75 per cent responded. At 5.43am Called out Chief Fire Officer Redman requested the aid of firefighting tugs. The Britannia Towing Co. mobilised the tugs *Queensforth*, *Herculaneum*, *Majestic* and *Gower*. Two of these were used for cooling the ships hull, while the other two nosed the *Duchess* toward the jetty, as she was showing signs of drifting.

A view of the Alexandra Road fire station, next door to the library. Outside is the fire brigade staff car, a Vauxhall Wyvern, KWN 243. (Mr Edwin Brimble)

Scenes of the aftermath of the collapse of several buildings in Prince of Wales Road, Swansea, on 9 September 1950, where seven people lost their lives. These photographs show the debris and remains that collapsed into the Strand, near Cwm Road in the Hafod. (Swansea fire brigade)

Most of the ships crew were dazed and confused, and were taken to the Swansea Sailors Home while the initial firefighting operations were in progress. However, cries for help were heard from the vessel, which prompted Sub Officer Gene Stratton, with firemen Ernie Gabriel and Len Harries, to ship a 35ft ladder to the captain's bridge. They smashed a heavy glass window on the port side to release Captain Tsesmelis and Captain Kaminis, who had become trapped when an explosion distorted the superstructure of the ship. The firefighting operation continued through the night, until at 7.35am a message was sent by CFO Redman saying that the fire was under control and showing signs of abating. At 9.25am this was followed by a 'stop message', when foam jets were substituted by water for cooling. A search for the missing crew members was instigated, and three bodies were found on the bridge deck. Another was buried under debris near the pump house, while a fifth was in the wreckage of the centre castle area.

At approximately 10.25am an explosion occurred which involved the No.5 tank, and six members of

DAVIES, MAY, COLLERTON, WALKEY, GABRIEL.

WHILST SEARCH TAKING PLACE ⟶

THREE DAYS OF TORRENTIAL RAIN CAUSE THIS COLLAPSE
I — SMOKEY COLLERTON (FIREMAN) 1st TURN-OUT ON SCENE
SPENT 6 HOURS ON RECOVERY OF VICTIMS, PERSONALLY
RECOVED (DEAD) THE BODY OF BEAUTIFUL (GIRL CHILD) BURIED IN DEBRIS ENCLOSED IN HER BEDDING

The Laurels, which along with other properties was demolished to make way for the Grove Place fire brigade HQ, pictured in 1925. (Swansea Reference Library)

the Swansea brigade were injured. CFO Redman was blown from the deck on to the jetty and into the dock but escaped uninjured. Leading Fireman Harry Davies and firemen John Neill, Amos May, Jim Collerton, Terry Walkey and Ernie Gabriel were not so lucky and all suffered burns. The worst affected was Fireman Ernie Gabriel, who was detained in hospital for several weeks.

A sixth body was retrieved from the vessel, but the seventh and final crewman's body was not located until nearly two weeks later, bringing to an end Swansea's worst ever ship disaster. The *Atlantic Duchess*, although broken in two, was eventually towed back to Hartlepool, where she was rebuilt. During the fire, there had been serious concern for a further three tankers, the *Four Lakes*, the *General Sand Morton* and the *Mesa Verdi*, all of which were moored close by. During the course of the firefighting they were all moved away from the blaze.

The ships Greek owners, S. Livanos & Co. Ltd, on 19 March, forwarded a cheque for 100 guineas to CFO Redman, to distribute among the personnel who attended the fire. The actual wording read: 'As an expression of their gratitude they have been instructed to send you the cheque for 100 guineas, who, by the very courageous work saved valuable lives and prevented an even greater disaster.' The note was signed on behalf of the company by their London office.

It is interesting to note that, after the installation of British Petroleum at the docks and the building of its refinery at Llandarcy, the first oil tanker to enter the Queen's Dock at Swansea was the SS *Scottish American* on 15 March 1921, when it delivered a cargo of 250,000 gallons of oil from Florida.

Following the fire, Chief Fire Officer Redman was inundated with letters from brigades all over Britain, conveying their congratulations and requesting information about the fire. In June, Redman was presented with the King's Police and Fire Service Medal for distinguished service.

In March 1951, the Minister of Local Government and Planning confirmed a compulsory purchase order for the site of the Laurels, the cottage Tyn yr Graig and numbers 11 to 14 Grove Place, for the erection of the new Swansea fire brigade headquarters and fire station. In August 1951 the Fire Brigade Committee completed the plans for demolishing and clearing the Grove Place site.

His Majesty's Chief Inspector for Fire Brigades, Mr H.M. Smith, revealed in a report how concerned he was about fire brigade premises and appliances.

He suggested that over 50 per cent of fire stations in commission were unsuitable, remarking that some were 'no more than leaky barns, or corrugated sheds'. The appliances, the majority of which were inherited from the war years, were nothing more than makeshift, having been hastily adapted for emergency use.

Possibly as a result of this statement, Dennis Bros of Guildford designed new prototype fire engines. One such engine was the Dennis F12, which was fitted with a Rolls-Royce eight-cylinder petrol engine, a 1000 gallon per minute pump and a demountable 50ft Morris escape ladder. With its enclosed crew cab, the F12 was one of the largest coach-built appliances produced at Guildford after 1951. The Swansea brigade, although still involved with the aftermath of the *Atlantic Duchess,* took delivery of their first Dennis F12, GWN 800, on 11 February 1951. The new engine was stationed at the central station in Alexandra Road and replaced the old ex-NFS Bedford, FYH 125.

In October 1951 the Swansea brigade joined others across the country in a 'work to rule', attending

The Atlantic Duchess *after the fire which engulfed her at Swansea's Queen's Dock on 2 February 1951. Seven crew members lost their lives and six others were injured, one severely.* (Alan Fox, Alan Davies and Swansea fire brigade) SMOKEY COLLERTON, ESCAPED BY SLIDING DOWN THIS LADDER - BURNED IN THE EXPLOSION.

Swansea fire brigade after breathing apparatus training in 1951. Standing (left to right): C. Jones, J. West, L. Harries and J. Lewis. Kneeling: G. Roderick, R. Daniels, Leading Fireman B. Ace and Bryn Williams. (C.Jones and B. Williams)

only emergency calls and carrying out only 'essential work' to keep appliances and equipment in a state of readiness. The boycott was a protest about fire brigade pay and conditions.

The site earmarked for the new fire brigade HQ was by this time all but cleared. However, Grove Place was at the foot of Mount Pleasant Hill, and in order to facilitate the work, the embankment, above which was Mount Pleasant Drive, had to be shored up. From the outset this posed serious problems. The initial contractor withdrew his tender because of the difficulties. Apparently there was a shortage of steel, and the original recommendation for reinforced concrete for the retaining wall was substituted for mass concrete faced with brick. Because of this shortage of steel and the enormity of the proposed expenditure, the building of Swansea's new fire brigade HQ was delayed by the Home Office until June 1953. As the site was secured, cleared and the enormous retaining wall completed, all of which had already cost around £20,000, it was felt locally that

This Dennis F12 pump escape, GWN 800, was delivered to the Swansea fire brigade during the days preceding the Atlantic Duchess fire in February 1951. It is seen here at Bracelet Bay in the Mumbles. (Mrs Jenkins) "SMOKY" COLLERTON WAS THE 1ST DRIVER TO TAKE THIS MACHINE TO A "FIRE CALL"

South Wales fire brigade contingent ready to depart for the east coast floods in February 1953. Swansea members included Les Harries, Ken Morgan, Terry Walkey, Bryn Williams and Leading Fireman Harry Davies. They were posted to Cambridgeshire. (Alan Davies, Ken Morgan and Bryn Williams)

the erection of the new HQ ought to go ahead. Following a meeting with Sir Hugh Lucas Tooth, the Under Secretary for the Home Office, Swansea's MP Percy Morris was told that a definite date for the commencement of the building would be a priority as soon as the steel and labour situation improved.

In February 1953 the east coast of England suffered incredible flood damage. The Swansea fire brigade, as well as other brigades from all over Wales and other parts of Britain, sent a contingent of firemen to assist with the clean-up operation. The Swansea contingent consisted of Leading Fireman Harry Davies, Ken Morgan, Terry Walkey, Bryn Williams and Les 'Bomber' Harris. They met the other Welsh brigades at Forge Lane in Newport, and

from there they were escorted by police to Haddenham in Cambridgeshire, where they were billeted.

South Wales fire appliances lined up in Forge Lane, Newport, awaiting orders to move for the east coast floods.

The 1950s was a busy decade for the Swansea fire brigade. Six years into its new role as a fire and rescue service, it had attended two of Swansea's worst disasters and sent personnel to assist in dealing with the east coast floods. More was to come, however. On 17 January 1954, the 8,128-ton British naval tanker *Wave Victor*, bound for Fawley in Southampton, sent out an SOS message. The first three radio messages

Swansea's firefighting tug, the Nirumand, *seen here lying alongside the RFA tanker* Wave Victor *in the Mumbles Roads. The* Nirumand *took a crew of Swansea firemen out to the stricken tanker on 17-18 January 1954.*

South Wales fire crews awaiting further orders at Haddenham, near Ely in Cambridgeshire.

picked up by an off-duty Swansea fireman, Karl Kostromin, who had been indulging in his hobby of searching 'over the band' on his short wave radio. On hearing the messages he informed the Deputy Chief Fire Officer, Mr Clarke, who investigated and organised the brigade's response. The ship was nine miles north of Bull Point on the Devon coast, just off

informed the coastguard that at 5.24pm there was a 'fire in the engine room fuel unit', by 5.29pm they reported the 'fire out of control' and then, at 5.37pm, the message came that they were 'preparing to abandon ship.' The *Wave Victor*'s messages had been

The rescue of two workmen following an accident while they were demolishing an old hardware store at the junction of Oxford Street and Waterloo Street, Swansea, on 24 June 1953. (Swansea fire brigade)

Lundy Island. The ships master, Captain Frank Cecil Holt, remained on board and later sent a message requesting tugs with firefighting equipment. Within a few minutes of the fire breaking out, 15ft flames had been seen by the Devon coastguard. Fortunately it was a calm moonlit evening, and lifeboats from Appledore, Ilfracombe and Minehead went to the aid of the stricken tanker, along with two merchant ships, the tanker *Pass of Leny* and the *Findhorn,* who were approximately nine miles away.

At 6.45pm the first reports of her sighting came from two small tankers, the *Moray Firth* and the *Pandora,* which reported heavy smoke issuing from the port bow. By 7.55pm the Ilfracombe lifeboat was alongside the *Wave Victor,* taking off crew, and by 8.30pm the burning tanker was drifting down channel in the direction of Lundy Island.

At 12.30am on January 18, a crew of firemen from the Swansea fire brigade, consisting of Sub Officer Fred Trew and firemen Ray Hill, Jack Fenwick, Trevor Harries, Harold Macklen and Tom Butler, under the command of Chief Fire Officer Redman, were alongside the tanker on board the firefighting tug *Nirumand,* owned by the National Oil Refinery. The fire in the crew's quarters was well alight, and the ship was described as a 'floating bonfire.' While the fire

The result of an explosion and fire on board the Norwegian tanker Olav Ringdal Junior *on 27 November 1954, when three crew members lost their lives.* (Swansea fire brigade)

was being fought from the *Nirumand,* the ship was taken into tow by the tugs that had attended from Milford Haven, Pembroke and Swansea. It was towed to the Swansea Roads, four miles off the Mumbles Head, and arrived there at 7am. As soon as the ship had dropped anchor, the Swansea firemen boarded for the first time. Using foam and water jets, they extinguished the blaze by noon. The Swansea crew all received commendations for their efforts.

Swansea's ship firefighting days were not over, as on Saturday 27 November 1954, following an explosion at around 4.40am that morning, a fire occurred on board the Norwegian registered 5,770-ton *Olav Ringdal Junior,* again at Swansea's Queen's Dock. The first 999 call that the brigade received was to a fire on board the tanker *British Surveyor,* and it was not until 6.45am that the name was corrected to the *Olav Ringdal Junior.*

The vessel had arrived in Swansea Docks on 23 November, with 14,462 tons of crude oil. This had been discharged on 25 November, after which she was moored at a 'lay by' berth, near the centre of the Queen's Dock, where she waited to be de-gassed.

After the fire on the *Atlantic Duchess,* a procedure for mobilising and combating ship fires had been devised. The first stage was implemented, which resulted in the initial attendance of a pump escape, a

Scenes of damage resulting from the fire on board the Olav Ringdal Junior *in November 1954.*

my 2nd 'TANKER FIRE'' '3 YEARS LATER'' - Recovered 1 Body'. (Relieved on job after 8 hours.)

Major pump, a foam tender and trailer pump from Swansea, a Major pump and trailer pump from Morriston, and, under the mutual aid scheme, a Major pump from Neath and a foam lorry from Port Talbot, plus two foam tenders from the National Oil Refinery. Along with these came the firefighting tug *Nirumand*. The officer in charge, until the arrival of Chief Fire Officer Redman, was Station Officer Jack Fox.

Land appliances were useless as the tanker was moored in the centre of the dock, so the firemen had to board the *Nirumand* and direct her foam monitors. A gale force wind was blowing, which seriously affected the *Nirumand*'s navigation. To alleviate this, two tugs, the *Neath* and the *Waterloo* were brought in, to stabilise the *Nirumand*.

An explosion had taken place in the proximity of Nos 8 and 9 tanks as well as Nos 4 and 5 wing tanks of the *Olav Ringdal*. The vessel was thus a serious hazard, as she was not 'gas free'. The undamaged tanks contained highly explosive gas. Firefighting was extremely dangerous, and the explosion had ripped a gaping hole in the ship, as well as lifting her decking. Although the initial firefighting had taken place from the *Nirumand* tug, when the opportunity arose, fire crews were sent aboard with cooling jets. They continued fighting the flames throughout the night, until the outbreak was eventually extinguished at 2.00pm. Crews remained at the scene until 30 November.

Most of the ship's crew had been on board at the time of the explosion, and although they had mostly been either rescued from the vessel or from the dock, the fire did unfortunately claim the lives of three young crew members, two aged 17 and another aged 25.

The experience of fighting the fires aboard the *Atlantic Duchess* and the *Olav Ringdal Junior* enabled Swansea's chief fire officer, Mr Redman, and his deputy, Mr Clarke, to impart their knowledge and expertise to other port fire brigades all over Britain.

In April 1954, a tender had been accepted from

The official opening of the central fire station on 18 November 1955. In the middle of the photograph are Chief Fire Officer W. F. Redman, Deputy Chief Fire Officer L.O. Clarke, the mayor of Swansea, and Major Gwilym Lloyd George, Home Secretary, who performed the opening ceremony. (Alan Davies)

Looking toward the drill tower from the workshop end of the drill yard.

The front of the central fire station on the day of its opening.

commenced in June. Eventually, with all the difficulties finally surmounted, the transfer to the new station began on 11 November 1955. The long-awaited opening took place the following week on 18 November 1955, when it was officially opened by the then Home Secretary, Major Gwilym Lloyd George.

Some statistics relating to the Swansea fire brigade at that time were:

Full time personnel: 97

Population: 165,000

Turn out area: 38 square miles

Appliances: 2 Dennis F12 pump escapes

2 Major pumps

2 water tenders

1 foam tender

1 towing vehicle

1 emergency tender

3 staff cars

1 utility van

1 motor cycle combination

2 auxiliary fire service EPs

2 auxiliary fire service motor cycles.

Staverton Builders of Totnes in Devon, for the building of the new fire brigade HQ in Grove Place, at an estimated cost of £104,000. Building

The new Grove Place fire brigade HQ was to

Swansea fire brigade's 'Big 6' Dennis fire engine, parked up after drills on the opening day in November 1955.

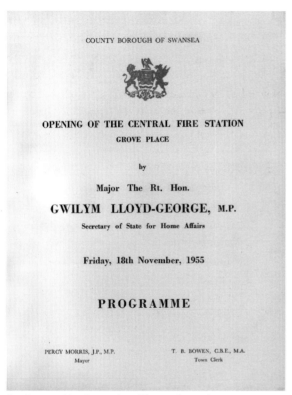

COUNTY BOROUGH OF SWANSEA

OPENING OF THE CENTRAL FIRE STATION

GROVE PLACE

by

Major The Rt. Hon.

GWILYM LLOYD-GEORGE, M.P.

Secretary of State for Home Affairs

Friday, 18th November, 1955

PROGRAMME

PERCY MORRIS, J.P., M.P.
Mayor

T. B. BOWEN, C.B.E., M.A.
Town Clerk

Brochure marking the opening of the new fire station.

The new control room on 18 November 1955. (Mrs Jenkins) and *the empty appliance room of the new central fire station, awaiting the arrival of the fire appliances.* (Mrs Jenkins)

The drill tower of the central fire station under construction, 1955. (Mrs Jenkins)

Swansea central fire station in the 1980s. (Gary Williams)

incorporate a seven-bay appliance room, a control room, offices, dormitories, a mess room, integral workshops and a kit room. Also incorporated were hose-drying facilities and a hose repair room. The station's dominating feature was the famous retaining wall at the rear, which overlooked a purpose-built drill yard and practice tower.

Another of Swansea's historic fires, described by the local press as 'the biggest since the Blitz' occurred on 25 July 1956. A 999 call was received at fire control at 12.47pm, informing them of a serious fire at the Kardov flour warehouse in Cambrian Place, near Swansea's South Dock. On their arrival the brigade were confronted with a mass of flames issuing from the windows on the top floor, as well as large volumes of thick black smoke darkening the surrounding area. The fire, which had started in the packing department, soon spread throughout the building,

*Think 15th from
TOP Row (LEFT)
(NEXT TO John Niel)*

Swansea fire brigade's official photo-call in February 1956. (Alan Davies and Swansea fire brigade)

Part of the opening day drills. Firemen wearing breathing apparatus. (Mrs Jenkins)

A floodlit central fire station at Grove Place, Swansea, in October 1956, when the station was approaching its first anniversary.

and the fire hydrants in the vicinity were unable to cope with the demand for water from the pumping appliances. Under the orders of Deputy Chief Fire Officer Clarke, a Major pump was set into the nearby South Dock. With five pumps, the turntable ladder and a salvage tender, as well as two pumps from the Glamorgan brigade, the firemen worked furiously from ladders as well as from ground level in an attempt to prevent the fire from spreading to the adjoining Customs and Excise Building. However, within a short space of time the roof collapsed. Luckily, all firemen had been withdrawn from the building, as the floors were also showing signs of overloading. The amount of water that had been absorbed by the building led to cracks appearing in the walls of the building, causing the firemen to combat the blaze from a safer distance, at the front as well as from the Cambrian Yard at the rear. At the height of the blaze no fewer than 14 jets were in use. Firemen remained at the scene, fighting the blaze throughout the day and well into the night and the following day. At one time, due to sparks from the Kardov fire, a blaze broke out at Easton's timber yard at the South Dock. This was extinguished by the attendance of a further two pumps that had been 'standing by' at the central fire station.

A fire that tested the brigade's efficiency occurred on 6 June 1957. At 1pm the brigade responded to a

The Kardov fire on 25 July 1956. Jets at work into the top floor, from the major pump, the Dennis F12 1000 gpm pump escape, HWN 220. (Mr Harris, South Shields, Mr Spooner and Swansea fire brigade)

fire call at the Marks & Spencer Store in Oxford Street. Like the fire that had occurred in 1939, this blaze stretched the brigade. With thick acrid smoke issuing from the store the firemen donned their breathing apparatus in the hope of entering the building to locate the seat of the fire. However, this action was futile, as the intense heat and dense black smoke drove the firemen back. The top floor of the building was described as a maze, and would have

been difficult to negotiate, even without the heat and smoke. The Swansea brigade had to ask for assistance from their neighbours under the mutual aid scheme, and pumps arrived from Neath, Pontardulais and Gorseinon. Even with this help the brigade had difficulty fighting the flames, for as soon as they thought they had located the seat of the fire, it would flare up again, just as fierce as before.

With no other option open to him, the chief fire

Opposite page:
Firemen dismounting an escape ladder on to the roof of Kardov's adjoining building.

Swansea's Leyland Merryweather turntable ladder getting to work on the Kardov building.

A collection of escape ladders can be seen, placed out of the way because the building had been deemed too dangerous to work in. Only firemen with jets could fight the flames. The person in the flat cap is Deputy Chief Fire Officer Mr Len Clarke, who directed operations.

Perched on the roof of the Kardov building is a gentleman with a bird's-eye view of the whole proceedings.

officer called for pneumatic drills. He hoped that drilling holes in the reinforced concrete roof would enable the firemen to lower spray nozzles into the building. This was achieved, and some 16 hours later, the brigade successfully extinguished the blaze. During the fire, 35 firemen required hospital treatment for sore eyes, from to the thick acrid smoke that had been given off from rubberised goods in the store.

September 1957 saw the brigade, in their capacity as a rescue service, called to extricate the driver of a Bedford van. While in the process of crossing the Mumbles railway line, opposite the St Helen's rugby ground, the van had collided with an oncoming train. The accident, which happened at 2.05pm on 6 September, trapped the driver, Mr Philip McGuire, being trapped by the legs in his van for seven hours. Oxyacetylene cutting equipment could not be used because of the spillage of petrol, so the brigade had to resort to using hacksaws and demolishing the wall the van was crushed against. Once released, Mr McGuire was conveyed to the Swansea Hospital by a waiting ambulance.

In response to the experience gained on the tanker fires at the docks, British Petroleum, in January 1960, took possession of the newly-designed 'BP Firemaster' believed to be the only one of its kind. It was a twin-hulled catamaran boat capable of being manoeuvred through 360 degrees, which could maintain a steady

position while in operation. It was fitted with nine monitors, seven of which could be manoeuvred in any direction. The highest monitor was situated on a

More water is poured on to the flames. Due to the amount of water being used on the Kardov fire, the Swansea brigade had to 'set in' to the South Dock as the hydrants could not cope.

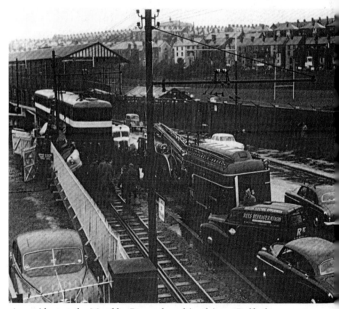

An accident at the Mumbles Bay coal yard involving a Bedford van and the Mumbles train on 6 September 1957. The driver of the van, Mr Philip McGuire, was trapped for seven hours before he was finally cut free by Swansea fire brigade personnel. The appliances in the photograph are pump escape 2, a Dennis F12, HWN 220, and the Bedford emergency tender OCY 22. (South Wales Evening Post)

Firemen attempting to gain access to the Kardov building from the Cambrian Yard at the rear.

Opposite page:
The BP Firemaster, a firefighting catamaran designed by BP for use at Swansea Docks, which arrived at Swansea in 1961. The first time it was used was at the British Flag *tanker fire on 8 December 1965.* (Swansea fire brigade)

Pump escape ladder drills at Swansea central fire station in 1963. (Gregory Davies, son of Dennis Davies, ex-SFB)

platform 40ft above the level of the water. The monitors could be used as either water or foam jets, with a foam capacity of 12,500 gallons. It was built by R.S. Hayes of Pembroke, to a design by the British Petroleum engineering department, and was to be stationed at Swansea's Queen's Dock. It was manned by a full-time crew from BP 24 hours a day, and in an emergency, a crew from the Swansea fire brigade, usually the pump escape 1 crew, would join it.

The 1950s had been an exceptionally busy period in terms of incidents attended, but the brigade had other problems to contend with. Nationally, there

was an exodus of firemen leaving to work in the private sector. The demands of firefighting and shift patterns were not rewarded with high pay, and this prompted many to seek better-paid work elsewhere. In the 1960s, an influx of new personnel joined the brigade to fill the gaps. The new recruits attended the Manchester and Liverpool fire brigade training schools for a 13-week period of basic training.

A group of Girl Guides attending their weekly meeting in the school room at the rear of St Andrew's Church, St Helen's, called the fire brigade on 27 September 1960 when they smelled smoke. On arrival the brigade were confronted by flames leaping through the leaded stained glass windows. Under the command of the deputy chief fire officer, the initial turn out of three pumps and the turntable ladder, all from Swansea, was augmented by pumps from Neath, Gorseinon and Pontardawe, and a turntable ladder from Port Talbot. With flames reaching an estimated 50ft into the air, there was grave concern for the church's conspicuous twin towers. An estimated 40 firemen were on the scene, and working within the building was hazardous. Thankfully, at around 11.15pm, some two hours after the blaze was discovered, the fire was sufficiently subdued for the firemen to install floodlighting inside.

The Swansea brigade's experience was tested again on 11 March 1961, when a general cargo ship, the 5,740-ton *Mataban*, signalled the Mumbles coast-guard using an Aldis lamp, informing them of a fire on board. The fire was in its cargo of rice bran, cotton seed, baled cotton and ground nut oil cake, and was thought to have started through spontaneous combustion.

On receiving the call, a crew of the Swansea Fire brigade turned out to the Mumbles pier, where they manhandled pumps and equipment aboard a pilot cutter, the *Seamark* and made for the *Mataban*. They

The Mumbles Blue Watch, 1963. From the left: Firemen Mansel Evans and Jim Sherratt, Leading Fireman Harry Davies and Fireman Geoff Walters. (Alan Davies)

were accompanied by the firefighting tugs *Clynforth* and *Waterloo*, as well as the Mumbles lifeboat. In its early stages, the fire, which was in the ships No.4 hold, was fought by the ships crew. On the instructions of the chief fire officer, the fire crew boarded and set to work extinguishing the blaze by the use of steam jets. The tugs by this time had the *Mataban* in tow and headed for Swansea's King's Dock, where, on their arrival, they were met by other fire crews and appliances. Once in dock, further crews went aboard in an attempt to extinguish the blaze, the heat of which had been so intense that the ships deck plates blistered. Thousands of gallons of

water had been pumped aboard, which resulted in the ship taking a serious starboard list against the quay wall. Dock workers were eventually employed to

The SS Mataban *berthed in Swansea Docks after a fire on board on 11 March 1961 while lying off the Mumbles. She signalled the Mumbles coastguard and a contingent from the Swansea fire brigade boarded the pilot cutter* Seamark, *then went on board the* Mataban *to fight the fire.* (Swansea fire brigade)

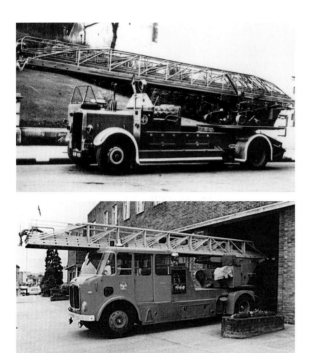

Swansea fire brigade's old turntable ladder, GLW 429, and its replacement, the AEC Merryweather, new to the brigade in 1964.

The AEC Merryweather was first used at the Manselton School fire on 2 March 1964. (Author's collection)

cut holes in the ships plates, which enabled the firemen to reach the seat of the fire, which was eventually extinguished two days later.

In November 1961, Chief Fire Officer Redman travelled to Buckingham Palace, where following the Queen's Birthday Honours, he was awarded the OBE. Then, in October 1962, he announced his retirement. His deputy, Mr Leonard Clarke, became Swansea fire brigade's new chief fire officer, with Mr Jack Clifford Fox as deputy chief fire officer.

The brigade's aged ex-NFS Home Office issue turntable ladder, the 100ft Leyland Titan, was replaced when it was accepted as part exchange for a new AEC Merryweather Type B 100ft turntable ladder, 511 HCY. The new ladder was described as the 'very latest thing in firefighting', a statement that was soon put to the test, when at around midnight on 2 March 1964, it responded to a serious fire at the Manselton School.

Another fire that required the new ladder occurred on 1 January 1965. After a call to fire

Left: Outside the appliance room of the Martin Street fire station in Morriston in 1962 are G.Roderick, Leading Fireman B. Andrews, Sub Officer G. Stratton, R. Daniels and D. Cartledge. (Gregory Davies, son of Dennis Davies, ex-SFB)

Morriston White Watch at the central fire station for drills. From the left: G. Roderick, J. Beare, R. Hill, Leading Fireman B. Andrews, R. Daniels, H. Macklen and D. Davies. The appliance is a Dennis F8 major pump, 933 LCY. (Gregory Davies, son of Dennis Davies, ex-SFB)

Swansea fire brigade's White Watch pictured in 1963. Back row (left to right): G. Roderick, R. Hill, A. Davies, B. Brown, P. Spring, –?–, R. Daniels and D. Cartledge. Middle: B. Jackson, F. Borton, G. Hoskins, B. Smalldon, Station Officer F. Trew, J. Beare, S. Edwards, L. Rees and H. Macklen. Seated: Deputy Chief Fire Officer J. Fox and Leading Fireman B. Andrews. (Gregory Davies, son of Dennis Davies, ex-SFB)

Fireman Les Edwards in the Dennis ACY 463, outside the old Southend fire station, Mumbles, 1963. (Alan Davies)

control at Grove Place, the turntable ladder was reversed into the station's drill yard, extended, and used as a water tower on the Mansel Griffiths motor accessory building, in Mount Pleasant Drive at the rear of the Grove Place fire station.

Just after 1am on the morning of Wednesday 8

December 1965, Swansea firemen Tim Tull and Gwronwy 'Rod' Roderick were on Watch Room relief at the central fire station, when there was a loud bang, which rattled the control room's windows. Sensing that an explosion had occurred somewhere in the town, their thoughts were confirmed at 1.17am

Scenes following the explosion and fire on the BP British Flag *on 8 December 1965. One crewman was killed. (Swansea fire brigade)*

officer, Mr Clarke. Also assisting were the tugs *Flying Kestrel, Brambles* and *Wallasey*. At 1.58am a message was sent to brigade control, informing them 'On *British Flag* at No.2 Jetty, Queen's Dock, ship full of gas, explosion taken place amidships and listing, BP Firemaster and four foam monitors in use, first stage help required.'

when a 999 call came in, informing them that as a result of the explosion, a tanker, the 11,000-ton *British Flag* was well alight alongside No.2 Jetty in the Queen's Dock. Immediately, pump escapes 1 and 2, the emergency tender and the foam tender towing a No.2 Dennis trailer pump, were mobilised along with a Major pump from Morriston. Travelling along the main road toward the docks, Fabian Way, the crews aboard the appliances were able to see that this was going to be a dangerous and protracted fire. The whole area around the tanker was illuminated, silhouetting the ship.

The BP Firemaster was used for the first time since its arrival in 1961, and the Swansea brigade's pump escape 1 crew boarded it along with the chief fire

With the first stage procedure implemented, a further seven appliances from the Glamorgan brigade and another five appliances from the joint Carmarthen and Cardigan brigade arrived. With the fire in the No.9 hold extinguished, and its hatch closed, No.8 hold was covered by three foam lines operating from the BP Firemaster. It was noticed that a large outbreak had taken hold in the crew's accommodation on the starboard side. Access to the area was through a bulk-head door on the port side. The fire was spreading rapidly via a communicating passageway between the port and starboard accommodation. Two water jets were brought into use by firemen wearing breathing apparatus. At 2.15am the chief fire officer sent a 'fire surrounded'

Swansea central's White Watch in 1965. Standing (left to right)*: T. Tull, R. Williams, J. Harries, K. Mills, B. Morse, F. Borton, D. Rewbridge, S. Edwards, B. Cann, D. Evans, B. James and D. Davies. Seated: R. Hill, A. Edwards, Station Officer H. Jenkins, J. Latham, J. Beare and G. Roderick.* (Gregory Davies, son of Dennis Davies, ex-SFB)

Chief Fire Officer Mr L. Clarke presenting Mel Dewey with a retirement gift on behalf of the Red Watch in 1965. Pictured from the back, in rows left to right: G. Petherick, J. Murrey, D. Thomas, D. Berry, D. Rees, V. Davies, J. Sommers, R. Crocker, W. Connibeare, S. Rees, L. McQueen, W. Martin, P. Robinson, I. Morgan, B. Williams, L. Harries, J. Neill, Station Officer P. Jenkins, D. Osborne, CFO Clarke, Mel Dewey, ADO Morse, Station Oficer F. Phillips and J.K. Thomas. (Swansea Archives, the Guildhall)

Swansea White Watch with the Dennis 'Big 6' pump ACY 463, before it was sold off in 1966. Seated in the appliance are (left to right): *Walter Martin, Keith Mills, Dennis 'Dapper' Davies and Rhys Daniel. Front: John Perman, Mike Davies, Alan Davies, Station Officer Walkey, Leading Fireman Bill Smalldon, Sub Officer Byron Parcell and Gwronwy Roderick.* (Gregory Davies, son of Dennis Davies, ex-SFB)

Home Office inspection at Swansea central fire station in 1966. Her Majesty's Inspector Mr A.V. Thomas is talking to Sub Officer Arthur Edward, with the mayor and Deputy Chief Fire Officer J. Fox. (Swansea Archives, the Guildhall)

message, which was followed at 3.15am by a 'fire extinguished' message.

During the course of the firefighting, firemen discovered the body of a Pakistani crew member, Jorhan Khan, aged 25. His body was found on the deck of the tanker. The only other casualty was another deck hand, who had received second degree burns. The last appliance left the scene on Friday 10 December, at 11.59am. During the fire 21 appliances and nearly 100 firemen had fought the flames.

The mutual aid agreement recommended in the Fire Services Act of 1947 also led to the Swansea brigade attending incidents outside its area. Along with the neighbouring Glamorgan County Fire Brigade, Swansea men attended a fire at 8.46pm on 18 January 1967. Appliances from Neath, Briton Ferry, Pontardawe and Port Talbot were also deployed, as well as a second hydraulic platform (snorkel) from Bridgend. The fire was a serious blaze at the Neath & Briton Ferry Co-operative Society Store in Windsor Road, Neath, which caused damage estimated at £250,000.

In May 1968, also as part of the mutual aid system, the Swansea brigade sent two pumps to another major fire. The blaze occurred following an explosion that injured seven workmen at the Llandarcy oil refinery in Skewen, near Neath.

A fire with tragic consequences occurred on 9 July 1967. Three children died after a house fire in Somerset Place, Swansea. The fire was discovered by one of the residents, Mr Clifford James, at around 7am. He procured a ladder and was able to rescue one of the children, a seven-year-old girl called Tracey, from the second floor. Before the fire brigade arrived in force, despite the intense heat and smoke, firemen rescued three-year-old Nigel Kirkham, who was brought out of the burning house and given oxygen in the adjoining Centre Hotel, only to die later in the ambulance. Two other children, Sharon aged 13 and her nine-year-old brother Russell, were found huddled together near the window, both, sadly, already dead.

The introduction of a new auxiliary fire service as part of the government's civil defence plan in 1949 had suffered in its early stages from a lack of response by volunteers. In April 1968 the government decided to disband the Civil Defence Corps. At a specially-convened parade at the central fire station on 10 April, the Swansea contingent of the auxiliary fire service was told of the government's intention in the presence of Alderman Jefferies, and officially disbanded.

Swansea's chief fire officer, Mr Leonard Clarke, was appointed as Her Majesty's Inspector of Fire Brigades in May 1968. Mr Clarke had joined the Swansea police force in 1937, following a period spent working as a mechanic with Jenkins' Motors in York Street. After a period of initial training he became a beat policeman, before being seconded to the fire brigade under Inspector Chadwick. His secondment had come about following an injury to Fireman Edgar West, who had broken his wrist attempting to start the fire engine on the handle. In

Swansea contingent of the AFS pictured following an exercise at Swansea Docks in 1959. (Alan Fox)

AFS personnel under supervision with a Bikini Unit at Swansea Docks.

Blue Watch outside the Southend fire station, Mumbles, 1968. From the left are Firemen A. Davies, J. Sherratt, P. Richards and Leading Fireman J. May. The appliances behind are the Bedford Miles water tender SCY 59, and the Dennis F101 water tender JCY 260D. The Dennis water tender was involved in a serious road traffic accident in the Mumbles some years later. (Alan Davies)

1941 he was promoted to acting sergeant, and gained a position at the newly-established NFS Staff College. When the fire service was nationalised in August 1941, he was appointed a company officer, and was commandant of the first fire service training school. After the war Mr Clarke worked in the Home Office Inspection Department in London, which resulted in his promotion to the rank of column officer in charge of Swansea and its surrounding districts. During this time he was upgraded to a fire force commander, before, in April 1948, being promoted to deputy chief fire officer of the Swansea fire brigade.

His successor, another West Country man like CFO Redman, was appointed on 1 November 1968. His name was William Frederick Dancey, and he had joined the Gloucester fire brigade in 1942 before doing war service in the Royal Navy. After the war he returned to his old brigade and was appointed station officer in 1953. In 1962 he became deputy chief fire officer of Eastbourne fire brigade, and after three years he was promoted to chief fire officer. Just prior to his appointment as Swansea's chief fire officer, he attended an incident that led to his leaving Eastbourne in what was described as a 'blaze of glory'. His last fire in charge at Eastbourne was a serious

tanker fire aboard the 15,000-ton Norwegian-registered *Silakund*. A news report at the time pictured Chief Fire Officer Dancey boarding the stricken vessel by means of a rope ladder swung over the ship's side.

Morriston's old police fire brigade station in Martin Street, which had been built in 1876, was replaced by with a new station with a three-bay appliance room in Sway Road (on the site of the present fire station). It was officially opened by Swansea's mayor, Councillor David Jenkins, on 14 March 1969.

The Sway Road, Morriston fire station, opened on 14 March 1969 as a replacement for the ageing Martin Street fire station. (Gary Williams)

The Mettoy's Toy Factory, at Swansea's Fforesfach Industrial Estate, suffered a devastating blaze on 10 March 1969. The fire seriously affected a large consignment of stock destined for North America. It broke out in mid-afternoon, and rapidly engulfed the factory, soon causing the roof and walls to collapse, as well as covering the whole area with palls of thick acrid smoke. The firemen's task was difficult and hazardous. Having to work in the smoke and fume filled atmosphere meant the need for a constant exchange of breathing apparatus. It was estimated that 40 firemen were employed in fighting the blaze, throughout that day and into the next. The Swansea brigade had been assisted by units from the Glamorgan county brigade. During the fire, the

Mangled and twisted metal was all that remained after the Mettoy's fire in March 1969. (Swansea fire brigade)

employees of the factory set up a human chain to try and save some of the stock, but the fire still caused damage estimated at £500,000.

The brigade's deputy chief fire officer, Jack Fox, retired in June 1969. He had seen service throughout the war, working with the NFS as a company officer, primarily at the water supply depot in Derwen Fawr. He was the station officer in charge of the first attendance at the *Atlantic Duchess* fire in 1951. His successor was another Swansea-born man, John Morse, who had joined the Swansea Fire brigade in 1949.

On 15 December 1969 Swansea was granted city status, which officially changed the title of the brigade from the County Borough of Swansea Fire Brigade to a city brigade. However, this had no significant effect on the fire brigade, which did not even alter its cap badge.

Tower Lane, which had become well known in Swansea after the tragic fire of 1932, was the scene of another serious blaze on Saturday 11 September 1971. This time the outbreak was on the opposite side of the lane, in the Mackworth Hotel. Now derelict, the hotel had been the constant victim of vandalism. At around 5.30pm that evening the Swansea brigade turned out with three pumps, two from central and one from Morriston, along with the brigade's turntable ladder and emergency tender. In the early stages of the fire firemen had entered the building in order to locate the seat of the fire, under the orders of Chief Fire Officer Bill Dancey, but not wishing to repeat the mistakes of November 1932, the crews were withdrawn. The premises were described as a 'death trap' and the turntable ladder and a hydraulic platform belonging to the Glamorgan brigade's Neath Station were deployed. Both were positioned

The remains of the Dennis water tender JCY 260D after the serious road traffic accident at the Mumbles which resulted in the death of Fireman Alan Sherratt. Leading Fireman Arthur Thomas had both legs amputated and two other firemen suffered injuries. (Swansea fire brigade)

Swansea fire brigade's turntable ladder in operation during the Mackworth Hotel fire on Saturday 11 September 1971. (Swansea fire brigade)

in the High Street, where they were used as water towers. Once again the street was closed to traffic because of the fire, and throngs of sightseers congregated.

Sub station 1, at Southend in the Mumbles, which had seen emergency use during the war and been used by the Swansea fire brigade since April 1948, was replaced. On 7 April 1972, a new purpose-built station at Fairwood Road in West Cross was officially opened by the mayor, Councillor Ken Hare. It had cost approximately £46,000.

The remains of the Dennis water tender, at Swansea central fire station's drill yard, awaiting inspection. (Author's collection)

The date of Sunday 24 September 1972 was etched into the minds of all Swansea fire brigade personnel. At about 10.30am, the West Cross appliance, a Dennis 101 diesel water tender, with its crew of four, had been engaged in hydrant inspection in the Limeslade area of Mumbles. They received a radio message instructing them to attend a fire at Langland. To get there the pump had to travel through the village of Mumbles, but just after passing the old Southend fire station the appliance went out of control, colliding with a tree and overturning near the Mermaid Hotel.

People in the village ran to the scene hoping to help. Brigade control in Grove Place, which had been informed of the accident, dispatched pump escape 2, with Station Officer J.K. Thomas in charge. They could not have imagined the scene that they were confronted with, which was one of total devastation. The appliance had totally disintegrated. Tragically, the driver, Fireman Alan Sherratt, aged 24, died in Singleton Hospital as a result of the injuries he received. The officer in charge, Leading Fireman Arthur Thomas, was severely injured, and both his legs had to be amputated. The remaining two crew members were released from hospital after treatment. Fireman Gerald Hoskins, aged 40, suffered a fractured shoulder and ankle, and Fireman Clifford Jones, aged 25, had a broken hand.

The driver, Alan Sherratt, was the son of former

The funeral procession for Fireman Alan Sherratt. Fire brigade members from all over Britain attended and are seen here marching up to the Oystermouth Cemetery. (Mumbles News)

Swansea fireman Jim Sherratt, who had retired in 1969. Alan left a young widow, Susan, and a son Peter, aged five.

After Fireman Sherratt's funeral, which was attended by members of fire brigades from across Britain, he was interred in the Oystermouth

The Torrey Canyon tanker disaster. She ran aground on the Seven Stones Rocks, off Cornwall, on Saturday 18 March 1967. Swansea fire brigade, as well as other brigades and HM Forces, attended to assist in the cleaning of the beach. (Cornwall fire brigade)

Cemetery, Mumbles. Forty years earlier another fireman, Gethin Harris, had been buried there.

The government's reorganisation of local authorities in the early 1970s sounded the death knell for the Swansea fire brigade. However, the brigade made its exit in a blaze of glory, when on 16 October 1973, the Lewis Lewis store in the High Street was consumed by fire. Firemen worked for two hours in breathing apparatus to confine the blaze.

Then, on 1 November 1973, the Swansea brigade,

Above: The rear of the central fire station and drill yard. Right: An aerial view of the front of the central fire station.

assisted by a pump from the Glamorgan County Fire Brigade's Briton Ferry Station, responded to a fire at Paul's Federated Building Merchants at the South Dock. At its height it was feared that the blaze would spread to nearby Gregor's timber yard, but fortunately, the firemen were able to confine the blaze. However, the builder's premises were totally destroyed, with the estimated damage amounting to £100,000.

As Captain Colquhoun, head of the fire brigade at the time of the Singleton Abbey fire in 1896, had said 'big fires usually come in threes.' The truth of this was shown by the Swansea fire brigade's third major fire in only a few months, which occurred on 18 February 1974. The brigade turned out to a fire at the South Dock, where the premises of Variflame Manufacturing Ltd, a company which

The central fire station workshops.

The central fire station drill tower.

made picture frames and photographic equipment, was already well alight. In order to subdue the flames eight jets were employed, and the Swansea brigade was assisted by three pumps from the Glamorgan County Fire Brigade.

The Swansea fire brigade, like other fire brigades in Britain and civilian groups, organisations and members of the general public, volunteered to

Scaffolding placed around the drill tower, to prepare it for demolition.

attended disasters. Some of these included the east coast floods of February 1953, and the running aground of the *Torrey Canyon* oil tanker on the rocks of the Seven Stones off Cornwall in March 1967. Fire brigades, troops and civilian workers were all employed in washing down the beaches in an attempt to clean them of the oil. The tanker was eventually bombed by the RAF.

The worst and most tragic disaster that members of the Swansea brigade volunteered for occurred on 21 October 1966, at Aberfan. Following a period of heavy downpours, a coal tip slipped down the mountainside engulfing two farm cottages and the Pantglas Junior School. One hundred and nine school children and five teachers were killed.

On 1 April 1974, the local government re-organisation which determined the end of the

Swansea fire brigade, was implemented. 'A' Division of the Glamorgan County Fire Brigade, which included fire stations at Port Talbot, Briton Ferry, Neath, Cymmer, Glynneath, Pontardawe, Pontardulais, Gorseinon and Reynoldston, amalgamated with the three Swansea stations of central, West Cross and Morriston to form the new brigade, which was called the West Glamorgan Fire Service. Swansea's central fire station in Grove Place became the new headquarters, under the leadership of Chief Fire Officer Bill Dancey.

The final demise of the old Swansea fire brigade came some years later in 1991, when the Morriston fire station, opened in 1969, was demolished to make way for a much larger station. Then, on 29 July 1992, the Grove Place fire station saw its last operational shift before being sold off to the police. A new two-bay Swansea fire station was built in Parc Tawe. Swansea had come a long way from the days when the town had been covered by pump escapes, one turntable ladder, one emergency tender, one foam tender, one salvage tender and a Landrover pump. Now the city is covered by one pump at Parc Tawe. What could be said to be the final nail in the coffin of the Swansea fire brigade came in August 1997, when the old central fire station in Grove Place was demolished to make way for a new police divisional headquarters.

Swansea's current fire cover is the responsibility of the Mid and West Wales Fire Service, which was an amalgamation of the old West Glamorgan, Dyfed and Powys Fire Brigades.

The rubble of Swansea central fire station following its demolition in August 1997. (Author's collection)